Tom Sainsbury is an actor, comedian, writer and social media star, famous for his Snapchat impersonations of characters such as politician Paula Bennett, wine reviewer Fiona and Gingerbread the Cat. Tom lives in Auckland, New Zealand, but was born and raised on a dairy farm in Matamata.

NEW ZEALANDERS

THE FIELD GUIDE

TOM SAINSBURY

AKA SNAPCHAT DUDE

HarperCollins*Publishers*

HarperCollins*Publishers*
Australia • Brazil • Canada • France • Germany • Holland • Hungary
India • Italy • Japan • Mexico • New Zealand • Poland • Spain • Sweden
Switzerland • United Kingdom • United States of America

First published in 2020
by HarperCollins*Publishers* (New Zealand) Limited
Unit D1, 63 Apollo Drive, Rosedale, Auckland 0632, New Zealand
harpercollins.co.nz

A catalogue record for this book is available from the National Library of New Zealand.

ISBN 978 1 7755 4168 4 (pbk)
ISBN 978 1 7754 9199 6 (ebook)

Cover design and illustration by Darren Holt, HarperCollins Design Studio
Cover images by shutterstock.com
Author photo by Andi Crown Photography
Printed and bound in Australia by McPherson's Printing Group
The papers used by HarperCollins in the manufacture of this book are a natural, recyclable
product made from wood grown in sustainable plantation forests. The fibre source and
manufacturing processes meet recognised international environmental standards, and carry
certification.

To my father, Ross, a real people watcher …

CONTENTS

INTRODUCTION

Hi guys! My name is Tom Sainsbury and I am very excited to meet you … through this book.

You're probably thinking, 'Who the hell is Tom Sainsbury? And why the hell am I reading this?' Well, those are fair questions. I guess I should do a little introduction.

So, I'm Tom Sainsbury. I've spent a lifetime in this beautiful country we call New Zealand. Or Aotearoa. I've spent a lifetime watching the people that populate this fair nation. Boy are there some wonderful characters out there – and I'm obsessed with them all.

I consider myself a scientist at heart. There was one stage when I would start statements with 'Well, as a scientist I deduce …' And the people I would be arguing with would say, 'You're not a scientist, Tom. Watching a dozen BBC nature documentaries and "having fun with static electricity" does not a scientist make.'

To those naysayers I say, 'As I scientist, I disagree with you.'

Now, as a scientist, an observation I made pretty early on is that there are a limited number of personalities in the world. There are billions of people out there, doing whatever it is they are doing, but there are *not* billions of

1

personalities to share amongst everyone. It is my opinion that there are people out there who behave very similarly to other people, even though they are not genetically linked. Am I making any sense? I feel maybe I'm confusing even myself.

Put it this way, I first noticed this phenomenon when I was 12. There was a girl at my intermediate school who wore heavy eye make-up, spoke in a husky voice, was always laughing and smoked. Let's call her Joanna, even though her name was actually Kristy.

God, I've just gone and ruined the anonymity of it all. Sorry, Kristy. From now on I'm going to be using fake names and sticking to them because otherwise I'll probably get into trouble with some of my nearest and dearest later in the book.

But anyway, Joanna … so, I knew Joanna quite well. She gave me my first smoke and I hated it. She laughed when I called marijuana 'mak' instead of the colloquial 'dak' throughout an entire conversation. She was very, very good at school and she loved corned beef.

During that year, the best science fair projects from our school were chosen to go to a regional science fair in the next town over. Mine was included – see, I told you I was a scientist. As a result, I visited another school (Morrinsville Intermediate) where I met someone we'll call Joanna 2. This girl behaved exactly the same as Joanna 1. She wore heavy eye make-up, spoke in a wry, husky voice, laughed a lot and smoked. She looked the same as Joanna 1. But that wasn't important. What was important was how she behaved.

I made sure I hung out with Joanna 2 at lunchtime, in the smoking corner of the field, and asked her some very unusual questions. What I was doing was finding out just how similar she was to my friend Joanna 1, and I deduced that she was very, very similar. In my mind, I grouped them together as the 'Very Smart Smoking Girls Who Love Horror Films And Jokes About Periods'.

After the Joanna 2 episode, I started noticing more patterns. The woman who worked at the greengrocers was boisterous and chatty, just like my aunty. The men my father used to yarn with at the local farming supply store were cookie-cutter versions of each other. They all spoke with a similar monotone and would mumble jokes under their breath. At school there was the First Fifteen Rugby Captain who was dating the Netball A-Team Captain. Then the following year would come along, bringing with it the next generation of First Fifteen Rugby Captain dating the Netball A-Team Captain. And you could barely tell these couples apart year after year.

Do people simply fall into stereotypes because it's easy? Or do given circumstances lead them to behave in a similar way? Or are there, like I first thought, a limited number of personalities to share amongst ourselves?

That leads me to question whether it is a terrible thing to group people into personality types like I've been doing.

Or is this just a sort of shorthand that we, as a society, have all bought into? Does it just make things easier? 'Ah,' you might say, 'that woman has a very specific haircut that has a longer fringe with a shaggy, short behind. From this, can we assume she'll want to speak to the manager when she doesn't get her way?' Or is that just limiting her in our minds? Is this kind of thinking, this kind of stereotyping, limiting our potential connection with other people? It's an interesting thing to consider, but I don't know the answers.

What I do know is I'm fascinated by these 'stereotypes' and have spent many years mimicking specific people, filming the results and putting the videos onto social media platforms for the public to see. To add value, I use various cheap nylon wigs and sweatshop-produced costumes that I buy from Kmart for under $10.

What I find most amazing is when a random stranger watching the video comments: 'Oh my god, this woman is exactly like my mother,' or 'This is my dad to a T,' or 'Graham, does this remind you of Granny?'

This always makes me feel like I've done my job properly. It makes me feel like I've captured the human condition in a tiny two-minute video. In saying that, watching back some of my older videos I think, 'My god, two minutes can be so long. Boring Tom! Why did you make this video so long? Hurry up and get to the point.'

Anyway, anyway, anyway … in the following pages I've collated all the character groups I've observed over the years.

They've been bunched into the various habitats in which you might find them, a bit like some sort of encyclopaedia of animal species.

I hope you recognise some of them and whisper to yourself, 'Oh my god, this woman is exactly like my mother,' or 'This is my dad to a T,' or 'Graham, you need to read this book because the character description of "Irritable Dad" is basically you, and you need to address some of your issues around that.'

In any case, I present to you *New Zealanders: The Field Guide*. I hope you bloody enjoy it.

DEEP SUBURBIA

Let's meet our first collection of wonderful
characters. For this, we'll be delving into where the
majority of New Zealanders live out their lives. It's
where they eat, sleep, party, booze, have shouting
matches, hide in their bedrooms, visit the mall,
go to the hair salon, judge their neighbours, live
out their various fantasies, fastidiously clean their
surroundings, or live in squalor. That's right, we're
heading into deep suburbia. From Christchurch's
Riccarton to Chartwell in Hamilton, let's meet some
good Kiwi folk in their natural environment!

THE DRINKING MUM

Let's start with one of my favourites. You'll see them at weddings, you'll see them at bars and pubs, you'll see them at work functions. They're The Drinking Mum. They just love wine, but they'll drink beer too. Basically, they'll drink anything, but wine does hold a particular appeal for them. It doesn't necessarily have to be a classy wine. Chardonnay is usually a goer.

They love having wines on the back deck as a collective of kids play cricket on the lawn. They're the kind of women who see going to the races as an opportunity to dress up and drink with their gals or significant other.

They like wearing tight jeans – if they can get away with it. Actually, even the heavier Drinking Mums wear tight jeans. They even wear tight jeans to special events. Their tops won't be tight, though. They'll be loose, especially around the upper arms. They'll also wear a thin gold chain and bracelet, and they'll have multiple rings on. They like a good wedge heel. On special occasions they'll wear high heels but, god, they love a good wedge and French-tipped toenails.

The early thirties see the emergence of The Drinking Mum, but they really come into their own from 39 to 45. Sometimes they'll get a new flourish of confidence in their fifties. And watch out if you're a single man because they are ferocious.

If these women do have a life partner, he's always at home, and she'll always refer to him as her man. 'My man back home', she says. Whilst she's five-foot-nothing, he'll be six-foot-seven. You getting the picture?

Ooh, they also always dye their hair. You'll never see a Drinking Mum with naturally mousy hair. Oh no. They'll have blonde with subtle streaks of honey, or brown with subtle streaks of honey, or block black.

I first came across the Drinking Mum type when I attended my cousin's wedding on Waiheke Island. My first encounter was with a corporate-type Drinking Mum who had just a hint of white trash. Like, she appeared very successful with her clothing and jewellery and general demeanour, but she couldn't completely separate herself from her slightly trashy past. You feel me?

I had noticed her with her designer jeans and jet-black hair straightened to within an inch of its life. She had a strappy wedge on and red polish on her toes – it was a wedding after all. She was wearing a black sort of chiffon top that you could see her skin under. It was gauzy and disguisey enough to hide anything she might have felt self-conscious about. Her nails were manicured and red, mirroring her toenails. I'm not talking tacky red. I'm talking rich red. You feel?

It wasn't until the speeches that I really took notice of our heroine. The MC asked if anyone else would like to say something. From the back of the room came a slurred 'I will!'

As our heroine made her way through the crowd towards the microphone, she almost toppled off her very high wedges. Her blonde friend, who was also a Drinking Mum, called out 'You got this, Karen!' I can't actually remember her name, but Karen feels good. Actually, Karen is a bit too bookish. Perhaps Charlie would suit better.

So, Charlie made her way towards the MC and his microphone and I could feel the audience collectively tense. She was drunk, and we'd already had way too many speeches.

She took the microphone and faced us. Being somewhat pissed, her pupils didn't look like they were pointing in the same direction. She started to pace up and down very confidently, then she pointed at the groom. Okay, so I should make a note that she used to be his boss. The man my cousin had just married used to work for Charlie.

She pointed at the groom, who was sitting at the bridal table and said, 'You! When you left my business I …' Then her head kinda dropped and I'm pretty sure, for a split second, she fell asleep. But then she came to, looked around somewhat confused, then remembered where she was.

She resumed the speech and it was painful. There's no two ways about it. There were in-jokes that even the groom didn't understand, and there was a sense that everyone watching thought she should just hurry up and get off the stage. Eventually she did, but not before giving me the feeling that she was deeply in love with the groom – despite the fact that her man (six-foot-six) was standing at the back of the venue watching the whole thing. But that wasn't the end of it.

Later, on the dancefloor, she was dancing away with her blonde friend and joyfully screaming out lyrics. Screaming away on the dancefloor is the Drinking Mum's absolute favourite thing to do. Anyway, she spotted the groom and made eye contact with him. Then she did a very convincing mime of spinning a lasso above her head and flinging it over him. She then reeled the imaginary rope towards herself.

With everyone watching, the groom played along. With his arms down by his sides because of the tightening lasso, he shuffled over. She danced very close to him. She then got into a dancing squat and simulated oral sex on him. With her six-foot-six man watching the whole thing from the side of the dancefloor without any expression on his face. At this point, I'll just remind you that she was simulating oral sex on him AT HIS OWN WEDDING RECEPTION.

I saw her the next day at the token post-celebration barbeque. She and her blonde mate were wearing dark glasses and sitting in the corner drinking bubbles and smoking. It was 11 am.

At one point, a cricket ball rolled over. She picked it up and tried throwing it back to the waiting kids. The ball left her hand at right angles and flew into the garden. She laughed uproariously and her blonde friend joined her.

If nothing else, the Drinking Mum is a lot of fun. No one could call her boring and, boy, can she put away the booze!

QUARTER-ACRE SECTIONERS

Let's face it, the good old quarter-acre section is still the dream for so many people. How wonderful it would be to have your own house with a huge section for the children to run around in, and lawns to mow every Saturday. Imagine growing old there until the children leave, then having to downsize to a unit or move permanently to the bach.

I remember talking to a woman who spent a lot of time in America. She loved it over there. 'Sure,' she said, 'Americans may be kooky and crazy and sometimes too much, but at least they're constantly striving for something and always working towards self-improvement. What I find so tiresome about New Zealanders is they are so complacent; their lives play out like clockwork. They don't look inwards and try to self-improve. All they're looking to do is buy a boat and a bach and be happy.'

Now, there's definitely two sides to this argument. Sometimes simpler is better. Maybe having humble dreams of getting that boat and bach takes all the stress out of everything. Or is it bad to reach the end of your life and not have addressed your deep-rooted problems and personality flaws?

At a party once I met a youngish couple, who were friends of friends. Let's call them Emily and Michael. They had both just done their OE, which entailed venturing to Europe, working in pubs, doing Contiki tours, running with the bulls, taking part in that tomato-throwing thing, working at more pubs, then flying back to New Zealand to settle down.

Michael shrugged at me. 'Yeah, we're twenty-eight now. It's time to pop out a couple of sprogs and settle down.'

Sprogs? That term has always stood out to me as peculiar. What an interesting way to describe your beloved children.

As the years progressed, I saw this couple maybe twice a year at various parties and they became interesting character studies. They would often reference how 'old we're getting'. They would leave parties early, and I often got a sense that they didn't really want to be there in the first place. It felt like socialising was an obligation with them. They would pre-empt their exit by saying something about not being able to drink like they used to and wanting to get home before midnight because they were 'nanas'.

At one party I had hurt my back and had to walk around leaning backwards. When Michael saw me, he said it was because I was getting old. We were in our early thirties. At another party, I overheard him talking about saving for his retirement.

Emily did indeed get pregnant with her first sprog. She would attend parties where she was forever rubbing her stomach and only ever talking about her pregnancy and impending motherhood. She was all over social media all the time. They even got a photo together, all three of them.

Dad, Mum and baby in the distended belly. Of course, it was in black and white.

The first sprog came out. A girl. Two years later they had a son. Then, surprise! They had a third child – another son.

Emily shared photos of the kids on social media and would get Michael into the photos as much as possible. He would feature in the pillow fort with the kids or he would be snoozing on the couch with the babe curled up on his naked chest. She would share articles and posts about the trials of motherhood with captions like 'ALL. THE. YESSES.'

All the kids had professional photo shoots done. The boys in dusty blue and little brown corduroy pants, and the baby girl with a pink headband around her bald head.

Michael worked out at the gym a fair bit to combat 'getting old'. He warned me about my metabolism slowing down. He was 33 at the time. He was big into DIY around the house. They were constantly doing the place up, making time-lapse videos of themselves painting a wall with face masks on, or of them constructing a treehouse for their kids. There was always a follow-up video of the kids reacting to seeing their new treehouse for the first time.

Their section was humungous. I don't know how they could've afforded it. But they *were* very sensible people and they had worked in the same jobs forever, so I guess it made sense.

Then they really did get old. Like, prematurely old. It almost happened overnight. He suddenly had very wispy hair and a pot belly despite all his gym going. She cut her hair short and wore mum jeans and cardigans. (They would've been about 37 at this point.) It was almost like they had willed this on themselves.

Then things started to go a bit haywire. I had it on very good authority that he had an affair with a woman at work. Emily never overtly said as much on social media, but she would share posts and videos about healing and forgiveness. They got through that bump, but then he did it again a year later. She moved in with her parents and everything seemed to fall apart.

I saw each of them individually a year after it all went down. They'd have been in their early forties but looked 10 years older from all the stress of it.

I bumped into Emily in the supermarket. She had very deep lines around her sallow face. She told me her ex-husband was an absolute psycho as she rolled her eyes and shook her head. She clearly wanted to give me the details and I was so ready to indulge her. I had finally found something interesting about her.

She surmised that it was ultimately good that the marriage fell apart. He hadn't been right for her. If only she had known that from the beginning! They got together too young, that was their problem, she told me. Plus, he was a psychopath.

I was walking through the streets of Wellington when I ran into Michael. It turned out he'd moved there. He had nicer things to say about his ex-wife and looked like the weight of the world had been lifted from his shoulders. His hair was longer, and he'd seen some sun. We talked pleasantries to begin with.

'So, where are you living down here?' I asked.

He replied, 'I mean, I should've done it better. I know.'

I frowned. 'Sorry, what?'

'Oh sorry. Were you asking about Emily?'

'No, I was just asking about Wellington … but go on. Is everything okay?'

Then he launched into it. He felt like an absolute villain, but it was the right decision. He simply couldn't live that Quarter-Acre Sectioner lifestyle anymore. It was killing him. He hadn't wanted that life. In fact, he'd never wanted it …

GAMERS

Let's discuss the subset of the New Zealand population who are Gamers. By games I'm not referring to Scrabble, Monopoly or outdoor pursuits. I'm talking about video games or internet games. I think. I don't know. I don't get it.

The first serious Gamer I came across was a young man I'll call Tim. I should note here that the vast majority of them are men. He told me he had to have therapy to deal with his game addiction because he'd worked out that he'd spent one third of the previous year playing this one particular fantastical quest video game. Let that sink in. One third.

That wasn't just one third of his waking hours either. It was every hour. He spent one third of the year with a console in his hand. The other two thirds involved eating, sleeping etc.

When I met him, however, he'd moved on from that addiction. By then, he preferred watching other people play. One time I watched him watching a video of someone in America playing a game online. I was watching someone watching someone else playing on their computer.

Tim religiously followed release dates of new games. He had even been known to queue for hours just to put his name down on a list to be able to buy a new game when it arrived at the store in three months' time. He claimed he loved these queues because they were the best place to meet likeminded people. Sure, you could meet them online, in the various fantastical worlds, but there was nothing like meeting them in the flesh.

Intrigued, I joined him on one such occasion. Across the board there was little musculature amongst the crowd. Everyone there fell into either the very thin or very flaccid camp. They also all had bad skin, and quite a few I talked to were lacking in the dental hygiene area. But their enthusiasm was fantastic. I would love to repeat what they had talked about but, to be honest, I'm not entirely sure what any of them said. Most of the jargon went well above my head.

When we got to the front of the queue, Tim placed his order then waited for a gaming friend to do the same. This gaming friend – let's call him Raoul – wore all black. His black jeans were baggy and frayed around the hems, which almost entirely obscured his black shoes. He wore a black Guns N' Roses t-shirt partially obscured by an open black hoody. He was pale and had acne. He also had a long ponytail and was severely balding even though he was probably only in his early twenties. The wispy strands on the top of his head were pulled back into the ponytail. In short, he was a fantastic-looking creature.

Tim and I went to Raoul's place and his gaming set-up was similar to all the other set-ups I'd ever seen. His huge, high-back, black, pleather office chair had a real spring action to it. His table had a glass top and silver legs. There were countless hard drives and metallic boxes piled around and two large curved screens. I cast my eye over everything, noting the various food crumbs smattered across the desk.

Raoul offered to teach me how to play, but his teaching skills left something to be desired. I managed to get through a game but was none the wiser by the end of it.

I also studied one other hardcore player. Somehow, he was in a long-term relationship but things weren't going well.

'You know that cliché about the dropkick boyfriend who's a gamer,' he said, 'and the girlfriend leaves in the morning and when she comes back at night he's still playing? Well, I'm sick of that cliché.'

A few months later, his girlfriend left him because he was a dropkick boyfriend who was gaming when she left for work in the morning and was still gaming when she returned well into the night. He worked through the resulting depression by hashing out his emotions in various computer-generated battle scenes online.

The only female Gamer I've met was a dab hand at car-racing games. I was invited to an afternoon at her flat with three other boys. We proceeded to get high, eat the best crepes and play this particular racing game.

Her skill was enthralling. She held the console with the lightest of touches and barely moved the knobs. And she effortlessly won. The other boys finished shortly after, then everyone had to wait for me to stop crashing and make it over the finish line.

She had completely clocked the game after only playing it once or twice and the boys loved her for it. As there were limited consoles and not all of us could play at the same time, the one not playing could be found staring at her adoringly.

Suddenly there was a knock on the front door and who the hell should it be but my old friend Tim, the gaming addict. He was visiting our heroine's flatmate because he played *Dungeons & Dragons* with him. I chatted with Tim and he assured me he was still not gaming compulsively. Then, as we had a second helping of crepes, I listened as Tim and his friends had the most raucous game of *Dungeons & Dragons* I'd ever heard.

There's another character type, which is a subset of the Gamers, I wish to discuss – the Retro Gamer. I've known two in my time and have met two others. They're traditionalists when it comes to games. They love *Pac-Man*, the original *Mario Bros* and a game called *Missile Command*.

This subset seem to be real, dedicated fans of quirky pop culture. They'll have a Quentin Tarantino movie poster on the wall, but it will have been done in anime style. Their shelves are filled with figurines, but with a crazy spin — like they'll have a Mickey Mouse figurine but painted to look like Chewbacca from *Star Wars*, or they'll have all the obscure characters from *The Lord of the Rings* but all with huge cartoon-like heads and tiny bodies.

When it comes to the Gamers I've come across, I can't help but admire their passion and friendliness, even if their personal hygiene can occasionally be a little questionable.

KNITTERS

As far as I can tell there are two subspecies of Knitters. There's the older subspecies, who are just gagging for an opportunity to make booties for a newborn baby. Ooh, they just love the responsibility of it. Any whiff of a newborn and they'll be pulling out their knitting needles and perusing the wool store for the softest of baby blue, baby pink or pale yellow lamb's wool.

'That's right, my niece's sister's daughter's cousin is having a baby in June, so I just thought it would be nice to make them some booties.'

They shake off any compliments with 'Don't even mention it!' But if you don't tell them how much you appreciate the booties they've made for your newborn, they'll be secretly venomous about it.

The problem with this subspecies arises when two of them are grandmothers to the same grandchild.

'Honestly, Mum, it's okay – Jenny's mum is making the booties.'

'I can whip some booties up tonight.'

'Relax, Mum, the booties are taken care of.'

'Nonsense. A baby can never have too many booties. I'll whip some up. I honestly don't mind. Now … what kind of wool is she planning to use? She'll probably use merino, which is a mistake – and that would be so like her. Anyway, I've already got the needles out. I can whip up a pair whilst I watch *MasterChef*.'

Then there is the second subspecies of Knitters. I visited one on a trip to Dunedin. The path to her suburban house was broken concrete. I walked through the front door straight into the kitchen where brown paper bags of organic lentils and kidney beans lined the dusty wooden shelves. The fruit bowl contained gnarled organic lemons and a limp, organic tamarillo.

Walking through the living room, I noted the old quilt over the rickety, wooden armchair. The spring couch had sunk in one corner and a tabby cat slept in the hollow. The bookshelf beside the mantelpiece was chocka with Ursula

Le Guin science fiction books, alongside which sat a copy of Naomi Klein's *No Logo*. I started picking up the tell-tale signs. There was a very full brown paper bag leaning against a medieval lute with 'Mohair' written across it in black Sharpie.

I ventured into the bedroom where the Knitter in question was at work. She was seated at a spinning wheel that I later found out was called a Lendrum Original Double Treadle Spinning Wheel, which she'd had to get delivered from Australia.

Her foot was pumping the treadle whilst her hands were feeding wool into the top part of the spinning wheel. Her long hair, which had never seen a dye in its existence, was in a loose bun hanging at the back of her head. Her face was completely free of cosmetics. I noticed she was dressed top-to-toe in woollen products.

'I made them all,' she said, faux-casually with a shrug.

She paused the wheel. 'This,' she said, pointing to her brownish tunic, 'is made from Shetland wool and dyed purple with beetroot.'

I examined it. I guessed that it had a purplish hue, but I wouldn't have staked my life on it.

'And these,' she said, pointing to her brownish woollen trousers, 'are made with Lincoln Longwool wool and dyed yellow with wild fennel. And these,' she said, pointing to her brown socks, 'are made from Suffolk sheep wool and dyed red with raspberries.'

The tunic appeared warped and hung stiffly on her body and the socks constantly slipped down throughout our time together. The yellow/brown trousers seemed a treat though. However, she did seem to itch her legs more than the average person.

I asked her why she was so passionate about knitting and using wool. She explained that she didn't want to support any sweatshop or chain clothing store, and she was sick of using clothes for one season before they were ruined and had to be thrown out. She wanted to make clothes that lasted. Suddenly I felt bad for all the aspersions I'd cast upon her.

As time went on, and several cups of horopito tea (made from leaves she had foraged in the Botanic Gardens) had been drunk, I started to sniff a certain artifice about the whole thing. She loved being the girl who knitted. She loved being able to wince whenever someone mentioned anything she thought of as wasteful and inorganic.

She liked to make woollen gifts for friends and occasionally sold things at craft fairs. I attended one such craft show with her a few months later. She was selling a dozen home-knitted articles of clothing, which must've taken her hundreds of hours to make. Side by side on the hanger I could tell the subtle differences in colours made by the natural wools.

The craft fair was packed with alternative-looking student types and alternative-looking older types. The stall to her left was selling terrariums, which are glass jars containing pastoral and woodland scenes made from dry moss and plastic animal figurines. They came with an optional brown cardboard gift tag tied onto the jar with coarse brown string.

The stall to her right sold a lot of crocheted things – an octopus, a Chewbacca, even a road cone – badges of kooky designs and colourful, zany earrings, which looked like squiggly snakes or fern fronds.

The craft fair clientele had a lot of piercings. The piercings included a lot of septums and sometimes two studs in either cheek. They also sported fringes high up on their forehead. I'm talking a centimetre-long fringe and then long, curly hair at the back. Unlike our knitting heroine, there was a lot of hair dying going on. I saw two people with aquamarine hair and one with teal, and countless pinks.

The only food at the fair was cupcakes – vegan and intricately iced. Some were iced like vaginas, others were iced with 1980s pop culture references.

Our heroine actually ended up selling a brown (green) sweater and she was super chuffed about it. The rest of the clothing, she assured me, would be gifts for family members. I ended up buying a pair of socks. They were very warm but useless in boots because they kept slipping down. In fact, they're only good with a shoe that'll pin them in place.

KIWI CATS

No, I'm not talking about the wonderful Andrew Lloyd Webber musical without much of a plot, which is the cause of a lot of musical-loving children's sexual awakening as they watch anthropomorphised human cats in tights writhing around on stage. I'm talking about the fuzzy friends that live in so many New Zealanders' households, escaping at night-time to kill native birds then leave the heads on your doormat. Cats are such an integral part of our society that they are often loved more than our fellow man. They're sometimes treated as humans and their images are often shared on social media.

I believe there are four subsets of New Zealand felines. First, there are the neurotic ones. There is one that lives on my street that I've given the name The Crackwhore Cat. She sees you a block away and starts running towards you with a sustained, somewhat desperate miaow pulsing forth. When she reaches you, her demeanour changes. She becomes seductive and milky.

But when you go to touch her, as you presume that is what she wants, she leaps back absolutely terrified, her expression reading as 'What the hell are you doing?'

The second you retract your hand her seduction resumes. She rubs her face against a fence and purrs suggestively. You go to pat her again and she leaps away. 'What the hell? Don't touch me!'

Then it's instantly back to being seductive. A final attempt to pat her is met with a panicked scamper and a desperate run/scream away from you, then a leaping onto a fence from where she looks back at you with terrified eyes before disappearing over the other side.

These are the cats that also seem to have the biggest problem with the food you buy them. They'll eat only the triangle-shaped biscuits and will turn their noses up at square-shaped or circular ones.

Next up we've got the Chill Cat. These tend towards the portlier side and have sleepy eyes. They're forever slow blinking, as if sleep is mere moments away.

I knew one called No Heart Anthony, a ginger cat with big bones. He would comfortably sit in the middle of thoroughfares (halls, busy kitchens, driveways) without a care in the world. Humans would walk every which way, narrowly avoiding stepping on Anthony's soft toes. He'd watch them lazily, his only movement an occasional yawn revealing the corrugated roof of his mouth and his raspy, raspy tongue. He also liked lying in the sunny patch on the carpet or lying beside the heater.

Sometimes a human would try to engage him in activity, perhaps teasing him with a feather hanging from a colourful stick – a pointless purchase made especially for him – and his face would consider the feather with intrigue for three seconds then he'd look away and yawn, revealing his corrugated mouth roof and raspy, raspy tongue. The feather would then be rested at easy access for him, three centimetres from his paws. He might tap it once, then walk away to find the busiest thoroughfare to lie in.

Next up there's the Tiger Cat. These creatures are forever stalking around their territory, just waiting for an intruder, so they can puff up with rage and growl unearthly sounds that seem to get impossibly low.

The standoffs between the Tiger Cat and the intruder can go on for hours unless you stand between them and hiss loudly. Then the respective parties will back away from each other, their eyes still locked.

These cats love to slink, head down, brows heavy, eyes always looking, waiting. They also love to urinate. On everything.

You can try to befriend them, but you are clearly an annoyance. These guys also have confidence that far outweighs their size. They don't seem to realise that humans are 20 times bigger than them and can easily squash their little necks.

They also have no problem taking on dogs. They seem to be able to smell out the weakest of their canine counterparts, completely terrorising them into submission. We had one such cat. Well, he was my sister's. He was originally called Cleopatra, but when we found out he was male, his name was changed to Cleo, which … is just as feminine.

He used to lie in wait down the hallway and whenever one of us children would pass, he'd leap out and really attack us. Cleo caused many a tear and a wail, and seemingly only did it for his own amusement.

Then there is the Comfortable Pal cat. These beauties are very comfortable in human company and love nothing more than a stroke or an occasional play with a toy mouse, which they seem to realise is a toy but still go through the motions of catching and killing it.

There are two cats that live in the apartment below me. One of them, Una, falls into the Comfortable Pal category. She was supposed to get spayed at six months old but fell pregnant at five months. She gave birth to Stitch, a grey tomcat, who falls into the Tiger Cat category.

I see their silhouettes through the mottled glass door as they wait for me to let them in. Una loves jumping on my shoulders and staying there. I can lean right over in an attempt to get her to jump off, but she simply digs her claws in and keeps slowly blinking her sleepy eyes. She'll jump off eventually so she can check out the apartment, have a bit of a cuddle, then maybe she'll have a bit of a fight with me, but the bites are never too bad and the clawing is always soft. Then she'll leave. All of this occurs within a 15-minute window and it happens most days. Why does she do this? Because she's a Comfortable Pal.

THE STINGY KIWI

I think we can all agree that stinginess has to be one of the most unattractive qualities ever. Sure, it sometimes comes out of necessity, but, in my experience, it is usually those with the least that give the most. There are people who scrimp and save, those who don't go out because they're paying off a mortgage, those who cancel on you last minute because if they spend $5 on a coffee it means they can't pay rent that week. I'm giving these guys a free pass. I get it. Sometimes money can be tight.

The particular people I am talking about – Stingy Kiwis – are next level. I have it on very good authority that the people I am about to discuss are on very good salaries, so they don't need to be so stingy.

Let's call our one Chloe. She remembers every financial transaction you've ever had with her. She'll suggest that you cover the cost of the taxi tonight because you still owe her $12.57 from that time she shouted you a bus ticket five years ago.

If you happen to go on a road trip with Chloe, she'll pay for the petrol then five months down the track she'll say, 'Hey, do you mind paying for the movies tonight? Because I paid for the petrol when we drove down to Hamilton together five months ago.'

For Chloe, paying $12.57 for a bus ticket and paying for petrol to go to Hamilton was done out of begrudging necessity. If she can get away with not paying for something, you'd better believe she will. And she'll be very canny whilst she's at it.

Her favourite trick is forgetting her wallet once the bill arrives. 'Oh shit, oh shit, oh shit,' she'll say with a grimace. 'Oh shit. You know what I've done?'

The other members of your party will just stare at her or share grey expressions with each other. They all know what's coming.

'You know what I've done? I've forgotten my wallet.' Then she theatrically sighs and shakes her head, maybe even pats down her pockets or looks in her bag again, though she knows she won't find anything. 'I can't believe it. I hope I haven't lost it …'

At this point, you can toy with her a little. 'Oh Chloe, that's so terrible. Where did you last see it? Let's go there right now.'

'Oh no,' she'll say. 'I think I might have left it at home. Stupid me.'

A pregnant pause will then follow before some poor schmuck speaks up. 'I'll cover you.'

'Oh! Thank you so much. I'll pay you back. Just give me your bank account deets.'

Most of the time, the poor schmuck won't bother giving her their deets and Chloe will have got away with it again. She has no problem swindling someone out of money, but good luck trying to do the same to her.

Another one of Chloe's tricks is that she will always choose to walk home to avoid paying for a taxi.

'Are you sure, Chloe? Can't you just take the taxi?'

'Nah, I'll walk.'

'But that'll take three hours and it's already one am.'

'Nah, I'll be all right.'

Then you'll invariably choose to walk with her because the last thing you want to do is read about her grisly murder the next day. Three hours later, your thighs will be chaffed, and you will have run clean out of conversation.

I ventured to do some research into Chloe's background. When I heard her parents were in town, I made an appearance at her flat. The parents appeared very middle class and didn't seem particularly stingy. I was invited along to brunch, where they happily paid for everyone's meal, so it's not like Chloe was an apple that hadn't fallen far from the tree.

One day, I ran into one of Chloe's old flatmates. Boy, did she have some great Chloe yarns to share. Apparently, Chloe would get furious if one of the other flatmates left a light on when they were out of the room. Two of her flatmates got pneumonia over a winter because she was very disapproving of heating. Then when she left the flat, she took absolutely everything of hers with her – handle-less plastic buckets, ice cream that had crystallised, a broken three-legged chair, a cane mat that disintegrated when you picked it up. There was no way in the cold depths of hell that Chloe was going to let someone else have something for free.

Ooh and before I forget, Chloe also used to take multiple sugar sachets from cafes, so she didn't have to buy any, and her almost-bare pantry always contained McDonald's ketchup sachets. No surprises, her catchphrase was: 'Is there free wifi?'

The one thing I will say for Chloe is that she managed to buy her own house a decade before anyone else I know. It was cruddy as hell and was furnished with stuff she had found around the neighbourhood. Inorganic collection day was her Christmas.

Somehow the house had a cosiness to it. Sure, the backs of the shelves were rotten and, sure, the couch squabs had been heavily rained on before Chloe got her hands onto them, but the overall effect was quite pleasant.

I still wonder about Chloe. Does she ever actually enjoy herself? Is she emotionally impacted, always calculating how to square up ledgers with good friends, or does she actually get an immense amount of joy knowing she has wrung every single cent out of her existence?

THE RICH

I remember finding out my supervisor at Matamata New World was on $10 an hour. I thought, 'Phwoar! That's a goldmine compared to my $5.95,' and told my mother of my findings. She explained to me that the boss of the country's major dairy company made $20K a week ... my mind was completely blown. How could people earn so much? What makes them so special? And what do they do with all that cash, for goodness sake? So began my (very distanced and very bewildered) analysis of The Rich. Needless to say, I found out they weren't particularly special.

During my university days I lived and died by a wonderful organisation called Student Job Search. If you were strapped for cash, as I was on the regular, you could show up when their offices opened and ask for any job that was going that day – and get paid cash at the end of the day. That cash would then be poured directly into rent and buying instant noodles for the week.

One such job I got was a gardening gig in the Auckland suburb of Parnell. I walked there because my car was parked on the side of the road four blocks from my flat. It had run out of petrol in the middle of a nearby roundabout and I'd managed to use momentum to roll the car alongside the curb, then I'd just left it there.

I showed up at the Parnell house and it was palatial. The lawns were expansive. Monstrous phoenix palms ringed the property. I knocked on the huge door and was greeted by the old woman who lived there alone. Let's call this treasure Joan. She was a wiry thing with voluminous grey curls. She wore riding boots, a riding jacket and jodhpurs. It looked as if she was going horse riding, even though she lived in the middle of suburbia.

Joan set me to task pulling out the wandering jew from beneath a camellia grove. Every hour or so, she brought me refreshments of tea and cake. The cakes were from the local French bakery and they were divine. A few months later, I walked past said bakery and saw that all the pastries and cakes cost more than I'd been paid.

By the end of the day, I'd cleared the wandering jew. Joan was very pleased with my efforts, so offered to employ me every weekend for five hours.

The following week I discovered that the wandering jew was sprouting again, which fuelled my belief in the futility of gardening. It was on that second occasion that I was invited into the house for tea and French sweeties.

The house was ridiculous. Beautiful, don't get me wrong, with huge leather couches and chandeliers of every shape and size, and ornaments I could sell and pay my rent for the year. Joan was a smoker, which made me like her all the more, but her cigarettes were brown, thin and long.

She discussed her husband, who had died the day after his retirement. 'He worked like nobody's business,' she told me. 'He missed most of his children's childhoods. He told me he blinked and they were adults.'

She took a long drag on her cigarette and rubbed the head of her obese, elderly, greying black Labrador. 'Bought us all this of course,' she said, indicating the house with her cigarette-holding hand. 'But he just didn't know what to do with himself without work. I think his heart attack was from the shock of it all.'

Joan had a huge car, and, during my shift, she would drive away like a maniac, giving me an opportunity to nap on the lawn on her dollar. Every time she arrived back, hurtling down the driveway, there would invariably be a new dent in the chassis.

She'd clamber out and tell me – freshly napped – to take a break because she didn't want me working so hard. At the end of each shift she'd give me a cheque, which was a complete drag because in those days they took seven working days to clear. Invariably, I needed that money right away.

I knew she had cash because the chequebook was in her purse along with a wallet full of $50 and $100 notes. I kept thinking about getting my hands on that purse and paying for my lifestyle for months. I had got my diet down to a loaf of bread for $1 and half a dozen battery hen eggs for $2.10, and that could feed me for at least two days. All I needed to do was get my hands on one of those crisp $50 notes ... but I never stole from her. I promise!

As the weeks passed, I got more intel on her life. Joan had four children. I met two of them on separate occasions. Neither of them left me with a very good feeling. The son barely registered me and spent most of the time talking about selling the property and getting his mother into a more manageable home. It also became clear that he had asked his mother, or the estate, to fund a business venture of his. It sounded like it wasn't going well, but he was still holding out hope.

The daughter who visited couldn't get her head around me. Studying? Working as a gardener? Flatting? She loved talking about all her overseas trips, focusing on Switzerland and Austria, where she and her family went skiing 'whenever we can'. She kept commenting on the value of things around the house and talking about getting an evaluator in. She also wanted to discuss who was getting what when her mother passed away. This conversation was with her mother, which

I found a little tactless. She seemed particularly keen on the Royal Albert bone china dinner set.

Joan explained her children's behaviour by saying that people born into money simply expected money and it always worked out for them. Apparently, she hadn't come from wealth. She was plucked from obscurity by her husband, who was 15 years her senior, and she had grown very accustomed to her new lifestyle.

A few weeks later, Joan told me she was going away on holiday for two weeks, so my employment was suspended. When she got back, she called and left a message asking if I could come back and tackle the wandering jew again. For some reason, I never returned her call and I never heard from her again. I'm guessing that she's probably dead by now. I hope her daughter is enjoying the Royal Albert bone china set.

RUGBY FANS

You can't write about New Zealanders without mentioning rugby, right?

I'm the last person to write about the subject with any expertise. I played rugby at school for two years because I felt I had to, but I never went to training and prayed every Friday night that the game would be cancelled the next day. Then, if I did end up playing, I hoped I would be the reserve. I was the worst player in the worst team.

The first game we played involved us losing by over 50 points. Is that how you score rugby? The other team kept getting tries and we didn't get any. Anyway, on Monday the results for all the sports teams were read aloud at school assembly by the deputy head girl. When our result was read out, the entire school erupted into laughter, including all the teachers.

This could have been the moment – like in the films from the 1980s – when the coach turns us all around and we end up winning the entire championship. But it wasn't. We just went from bad to equally as bad. And I still didn't go to training even though I told my parents I had. I feel very sorry that I subjected the team to that.

A few years later, I had – thankfully for everyone involved – given up the sport, when everyone got excited about the Rugby World Cup. Some family friends, real Rugby Fans, were forever referencing 'our boys' and had bought tickets to Europe to watch 'our boys' take the cup, with the intention of watching every game until they did so. They even bought into the paraphernalia – the black-and-white beanies, the black-and-white scarves, those clacky things that you spin around and make noise with.

Long story short, they flew over to Europe, then the All Blacks lost one of their games and were out of the competition. When they came back, their resentment was palpable. The team were no longer 'our boys'. Like true Rugby Fans, they even tried to direct some of their rage at the referee on the day, but they just couldn't look past the fact that their 'boys' had disappointed them. They had flown all the way to Europe, for god's sakes, the least the All Blacks could have done was win the cup!

On the flipside, a few years later, I was hanging out with another avid Rugby Fan who we'll call Jake. This time the Rugby World Cup was in New Zealand. A lot of money had been pumped into the country to cater for it, amongst cries from the artistic community about how little funding they get – 'Why does ghastly rugby get so much money when my avant-garde performance piece about menstruation goes unfunded?!'

Anyway, Jake started off the season with all the paraphernalia – black-and-white beanie, black-and-white scarf, etc. He also wanted to paint his face half black, half white with silver ferns of the opposing colour on the appropriate cheek. Clearly, he should have used a finer-bristled brush for the silver ferns as they ended up looking more like blooming pohutukawa.

Jake also corralled his family into being big supporters. His youngest son was a huge fan before he could walk, let alone talk. He wore a baby-sized black-and-white beanie and a black-and-white onesie. His three-year-old daughter was subjected to the face painting. His eldest son seemed to cluelessly follow all the All Blacks players' careers and his 'heroes' amongst them were dictated by his father. His wife also bought into the whole thing, allowing a framed poster of Corey Flynn, the hooker, to be hung in the hallway of their house. She was also a huge fan of the black-and-white scarf and beanie combo.

Anyway, Jake was so excited about the World Cup. He was absolutely fizzing about it. He was counting down the days until the first match and was reading up on all the stats for the opposing teams and trying to predict how it would play out. He was desperate to have conversations about the competition, always wanting people's opinions on who was the best player, and what had been the best try in the previous World Cup. Jake loved it most when that person disagreed with him, as he could then have a heated argument with them.

Eventually, the World Cup began. The All Blacks won their first match, much to our hero's delight. Then they won the next game, and they won the next game, and they won the next game.

The next time I saw Jake he had a fixed smile. 'How are you feeling about the finals?' I asked him.

'Yep,' he said with a high-pitched voice and pursed lips.

'Do you think they'll win?' I asked.

'Yeah, no doubt. No doubt at all …'

And they did win. Against France. But I feel the avid fan was bored by that result.

'A thrilling game?' I asked him.

'I just watched the highlights at home,' he said.

I thought about his about-turn for a while. He'd been so enthusiastic, then that all just disappeared. I guess there was no mystery in it for him when they bloody well won all the time. Where's the thrill?

On the flipside of that are the fans of the ill-fated rugby league team, the Warriors. I had one friend who I was surprised to find was a huge Warriors fan. He had all the paraphernalia – the blue, red, green and white beanies with extremely heavy corporate sponsor presence.

I asked him how he'd got into it. He said he'd watched one of their first games as a teenager and he'd felt sorry for them. From that moment on he was invested in them winning the grand final. He basically wanted them to have the ultimate underdog story.

Decades had passed and they hadn't won yet, but he had made a deal with himself to support them no matter what. He was also terrified that the day he abandoned them, they would win and he wouldn't have seen his commitment through to the end. I suggested, perhaps too harshly, that him giving up on supporting the Warriors may just be the key to their success …

THE EFFORTLESSLY ELEGANT

There is a breed of woman who just have an ease about them. They can host a party and experience no stress whatsoever and still pull off the best event ever. The guest list will have been perfectly curated, stimulating conversation will flow, glasses will never be empty, and every dietary requirement will be catered for.

At the party, you'll get a chance to talk to the Effortlessly Elegant hostess. Even though she's busy getting all the platters ready, she'll still take time to chat with you and make you feel wonderful.

As you leave, she'll take both of your hands in hers and thank you from the bottom of her heart for attending. As you walk away, you'll feel like you're on cloud nine.

These women are also effortlessly fashionable. They can wear anything and look good ... but they never wear just anything. They wear understated clothes, which have been well thought out, that look so good on them.

These women have many male admirers but can skilfully extricate themselves from anyone's attentions without leaving the man feeling bad. Men love them because they've got such a beautiful, feminine energy but, at the same time, they can have a laugh with the boys. These women also have a lot of female friends because they're so good at listening. They're very sympathetic to all your problems even though you can't imagine them experiencing any problems of their own, because they just seem to do everything so well.

I call these women the Effortlessly Elegant, and they come in all ages because once you're elegant, you're elegant forever.

One of the first women of this ilk I ever met was my friend's grandmother. She was Fijian and she had a mass of grey curls, which were always held back with a polished wooden hair clasp. Her limbs were very thin and veiny but beautifully smooth. Her fingers ended with perfect nails, which were sometimes coloured coral, sometimes red, sometimes nude. She would wear kaftans or flowing dresses and she loved wide-brimmed hats. She was always smiling and would glide from room to room through her well-ventilated house.

Everything about that house was just right. The spaciousness, the well-chosen Fijian artefacts on the walls, the potted monstera plants growing in the corners of rooms. She also had an extensive garden filled with roses, lilies, birds of paradise and jasmine.

Vases of fresh flowers were throughout the house, and each arrangement was brilliant in its simplicity. Three bird of paradise flowers in a mason jar would look stunning. A single rose in a retro 1970s mug in the bathroom made you want to create a photographic essay.

All the food she served had a certain elegance to it as well. The fish was fresh from the market. The biscuits were never too sweet. The lemonade was always homemade. Speaking of lemons, the big wooden bowl on the windowsill containing three homegrown lemons was just begging for Picasso to come and paint it.

She had many grandchildren and they all respected her. In fact, she never seemed to have to put much effort in to get people's respect. Her very existence was respect-worthy. She even died elegantly. Apparently, she was sitting up in hospital, smiling fondly on everyone and waiting for all her descendants to be in the room. When the last grandson arrived, she simply blessed them all, slipped into a coma and was dead within the hour. She even made a beautiful corpse. As people howled at her somate (funeral) she simply lay there, her serene face having lost none of its glow.

Later on, I lived with another Effortlessly Elegant woman. She was an actress and men fell in love with her left, right and centre. A married man wrote a whole television series for her, so that he could see her all the time. Masterfully, she took the role but extricated herself from his affections.

She was often dressed by designers for her opening nights and other such events and she always looked amazing. At home, though, she would wear just one outfit – grey sweatpants and a pink woollen sweater with a silver button just beneath the collar. Even that looked attractive on her!

She was disappointed with me only once whilst we were living together. Our earthquake-making washing machine was beneath the kitchen bench. Once, I left all the plates to dry on the bench then turned on the washing machine. The resulting earthquake caused all her family heirloom plates to shatter into pieces on the floor.

Afterwards, she asked to talk with me in the living room. There I found her seated gracefully on the settee. There was a serene smile on her face. She said she didn't want to sound passive-aggressive, but next time could I remember not to turn the washing machine on when there were plates on the bench?

She essentially told me off with the upmost grace and poise. I felt I'd had a run-in with the Queen. I apologised profusely, then bowed my head and backed out of the room. And you'd better believe I never turned on that washing machine whilst plates were drying ever again.

You're probably thinking, 'You're painting a portrait of someone who doesn't exist. Surely these women have their own problems and screw up and have nervous breakdowns …'

Sure, they do, but they do all those things with effortless elegance. The Fijian grandmother's husband went into bankruptcy and took his own life. Her granddaughter, my friend, said she rose to the challenge, became the boss of the company and made it financially viable again. She even kept a photo of her husband beside her bed and would often speak of him, but she never let it get her down.

My Effortlessly Elegant flatmate once came home from a bad date and burst into tears. She cried for one hour straight, then pulled herself together. That very night she rang the man in question and let him know how he'd made her feel. Then she brushed her hair, got into her pink sweater with the silver button beneath the collar and elegantly moved on to planning a dinner party for the following Sunday night, her languid fingers moving across her phone screen as she dialled her first excited guest.

FLATMATES

During my flatting career I've had some wonderful living situations and I've had some terrible living situations. Sometimes I lived with friends, like the Effortlessly Elegant above. Sometimes I lived with complete strangers, like the young woman called Cloud, who was similar to actual clouds in that she never spoke.

When my flatmates have practically been strangers, I've always found it odd to share a bathroom, a space where you are your most vulnerable, with them. You're cleaning your genitals where they clean their genitals, and there they are, living their completely separate lives on the other side of the hallway.

There is a particular breed of Flatmate I have come across twice in my time. I've discussed this type of person with friends and they all have similar stories, so it would seem this is a stock-standard character type.

Picture this. The Flatmate shuffles into the living room with their dressing gown held tightly at the collar, their eyes half closed. 'Hey,' they say, 'I'm just trying to sleep. Can you guys maybe try and be a little bit quieter?' They then give a particularly pointed stare before shuffling back to their bedroom.

One of my flatmates once shuffled into the kitchen at about eight o'clock at night with his dressing gown held tightly at the collar, then he whispered croakily: 'Hey, I was just trying to sleep. Hey, did you drop something in the shower?'

I scanned my brain. 'Umm … Oh, yeah. I dropped the shampoo …'

'Yeah, cos I was sleeping, and it woke me up and now I can't go back to sleep.'

He then gave me a very pointed stare. A very awkward silence followed as I scraped butter across some toast, then he shuffled back to his bedroom with a world-weary sigh.

After living with him for a year, I realised that what he really wanted to say was (keep imagining him with his dressing gown held at his collar): 'Hey, I was just trying to sleep but I could sense you in the house.' Then he'd look at me with a pointed stare. 'I don't know, maybe you could sleep in your lavender Honda Jazz tonight?' Then he'd shuffle back to his bedroom with a world-weary sigh.

After living with that guy, I lived with a Flatmate who was forever lifting weights in the living room. He'd make a 'kss' noises at every exertion. This gentleman lived on whey powder and was very muscular, but he looked very unhealthy, with bad skin and dark rings under his eyes. Anyway, he and I lived on the top floor of the house. Downstairs was a blonde woman who looked like she milked goats in the alps then yodelled her way down into the flat. As far as I could tell, she lived off delivered pizzas – but the delivery person never came to the front door. Her bedroom had a window, which basically opened up onto the street. I imagined her waiting for the delivery person to arrive, then simply opening the window and beckoning them over.

After a couple of months of living together, I needed to use the cordless phone. I knew it was probably in the kitchen somewhere, or beneath some of the cushions in the living room, but I used it as an excuse to stick my head into the Yodeller's bedroom, where I saw a perfectly stacked pile of more than 50 pizza boxes in the corner. I have to admit there was something quite satisfying about its precision.

The three of us – me, the Yodeller and the Beefcake – had been living together for six or so months, very pleasantly, when we got a message from ol' yodelling goat herder asking us if it was okay for her friend to stay a couple of nights. This friend was between flats and needed somewhere to crash. Me and ol' kss Beefcake said that was absolutely fine.

Six months later, this friend of the Yodeller was still living in the house and she hadn't paid a scrap of rent. Let's call this new, temporary flatmate Kelly. When Kelly moved in with all her stuff there wasn't a spare bed for her to sleep on, so what she decided to do was erect her king-size bed in the foyer area just beside the bathroom/toilet. The foyer was tiny, and the bed took up the lion's share of it.

In order to get to the bathroom/toilet, you had to walk down the stairs, where you'd reach the headboard of the king-size. Then you had to sidle along the headboard and turn at a right angle, then sidle along the side of the bed, turn another right angle, this time at the foot of the bed, and sidle along until you reached the bathroom. Once you were safely in the toilet, you'd remember that the door was paper thin, so you had to deal with the anxiety of not making too much noise.

Kelly would be sleeping there every night (without paying rent) and if you needed to use the bathroom you had to slide along beside her, in her bed, as she slept, so you could be centimetres away from her sleeping body.

One night I had just been to the bathroom and was sliding back along the bed, headed for the stairs, when I noticed that she was stirring. I tensed and realised I had to make a snap decision – either I could speed off, or I could keep completely still and hope she fell back to sleep. I decided to do the latter, which was a mistake. I kept completely still, in the pitch black, not more than one metre from her sleeping body.

Anyway, she woke up and looked at me. She then jerked back, confused. I could've explained that I had just been to the bathroom. I could have explained that I needed a shower. I could have said many things but instead I chose to say: 'Are you having a good sleep?'

She nodded, sliding away from me on the bed. I nodded in return then continued on my way. When I reached my bedroom, I pressed my back against my door and questioned all my life choices.

Literally the next day Kelly moved out. I went to work in the morning and on returning found the foyer completely empty. She hadn't paid a scrap in rent or any bills. She was a freeloader but thankfully both Yodeller and Beefcake were aware of that and were both glad I'd got rid of her. All that was needed to achieve that was me being an absolute creep.

THE 'I'D LIKE TO SPEAK TO THE MANAGER' WOMAN

Look, I know this is an international trend, but we need to discuss this in a New Zealand context. We *need* to discuss our own version of the 'I'd Like to Speak to the Manager' Woman.

This type of woman really peaks somewhere around 42 to 52 years of age. What they all have in common is *the* haircut. It has a long, straight fringe, is parted to the side and is short'n'shaggy at the back. The fringe is the longest part and the rest of the hair would never be longer than about five centimetres. The hair can come in a full range of colours, though, and there are extra points for block streaks of blonde.

The costume of this species of women can vary but my favourite combination is white capris and a pastel T-shirt. In winter they may also wear a pastel polar fleece. It's up to them really. There's always gold jewellery, of course, and in the summer, they like to wear expensive sunglasses. There are extra points if their sunglasses fade from a dark colour on top to clear at the bottom.

These women are invariably mothers. They are also invariably married to someone of lower status, and they are (invariably) forces of nature. Boy, you do *not* want to cross them.

I was at Briscoes in the heat of summer and everyone was buying standing fans. There, in front of me, was this beautiful creature. Capri pants – check. Pastel top – check. Her hair was pristine, a chocolate fountain from her head with a variety of blonde streaks ranging, I'd say, from two millimetres to a good seven millimetres in thickness. Her sunglasses, sans rims and with a pink fade, were pushed up onto her head, forcing her extravagant fringe from her face. She wore pink lip gloss and a lot of mascara around her eyes, but it didn't do much to accentuate them. Let's call this woman Rachel.

I had barely registered this woman before realising she was furious.

'But I saw it advertised online for ten dollars less than this!' she hissed, not even attempting to keep her cool with the shop assistant.

'That is for another version of the same fan,' the waifish shop assistant tried to explain.

'Well, I can't tell the difference,' said Rachel, with an exaggerated sigh.

The shop assistant pointed out the various different features, but Rachel was barely listening. She was too busy rolling her eyes. Then she interrupted the shop assistant mid-sentence: 'Well, can I get one of the ones on special please?'

The shop assistant explained once again that the ones on special were sold out, but the stock was due in two days.

'I can't wait for that,' Rachel said, dumping the current boxed fan onto the counter.

'Would you like me to see if another store has one?' the shop assistant asked hopefully.

'No, actually, I wouldn't. I rang here last night to see if there were some in stock and I was told by someone that there were twelve.'

'They've all been—'

'I've had to travel for forty-five minutes to get here.'

'We can—'

'Actually,' Rachel breathed in, then uttered the immortal words, 'I want to speak to the manager.'

The shop assistant hesitated, then nodded. She shuffled through the door leading into the staff-only area. At this point, Rachel muttered 'Ridiculous!' under her breath.

She looked back and saw a queue gathering behind her, but she was unfazed.

Eventually the shop assistant returned with a lanky manager who was all smiles. He guided Rachel away from the counter. I wished so much that I could have followed them and eavesdropped, but that would've just been weird, so all I could do was stand at a distance, reading their body language – and it was not good.

Rachel was constantly shaking her head, gesturing wildly then dropping her hands down to make a heavy slapping sound against her capri-encased thighs. There was even one point where she pointed at the manager and leant in, narrowing her eyes to make them even smaller.

At this point, it was my turn to buy my fan. I bought the copper-looking one even though I, too, had wanted the one on special.

By the time I turned back, Rachel and the manager were making their way back to the counter. He paused the queue beside me and allowed Rachel to the front. He swiped his lanyard, hit some keys on his keyboard, took the fan she had been holding and processed the purchase. He handed her the receipt and whispered 'With the discount' under his breath, probably hoping we wouldn't all demand the same.

Rachel snatched the receipt. 'Thank you,' she said, with no joy over getting her way. No, she had got exactly what she felt she deserved and was only annoyed that it had taken so long. Maybe she had a confidence we should all aspire to?

I walked out of the store, closely following her (without being too creepy). She quickly took out her phone and I noted her manicured, acrylic nails. They were a chocolatey colour that offset her hair.

'They didn't bloody have any,' she said into the phone, her voice very clipped, as she headed towards her SUV. 'Yeah, well, I made them give me a discount on the other kind, didn't I? Yes, I got it. I said I got it. Now put Dad on.'

With that she got into her SUV and put the phone on speaker. She roared the car out of its park then roared it out of the carpark, terrifying every other driver she passed.

CRISIS KIWIS

As I'm writing this, New Zealand is in the middle of a four-week lockdown because a pandemic has swept across the globe. (What is this? Europe in the 1600s?) I'm hoping that we'll get out of this relatively intact.

Recent events have given me an opportunity to observe a whole new array of Kiwi characters, and I couldn't be happier to have had this opportunity (despite the tragedy that took place, obviously). They're essentially just everyday, normal New Zealanders, but when the right circumstances come along, we see a whole new side to them.

Suddenly humanity has had to pull together to stop the pandemic and New Zealand, under the leadership of our Prime Minister, Cindy Ardern, has acted boldly and acted fast. Cindy closed the borders and put us all on the aforementioned lockdown. Suddenly we had to spend all our time in our house. The only time we were allowed to leave the house was for a brief stint of exercise within our neighbourhood.

We were all relatively well behaved and did as was required. Many businesses closed for the period, causing a lot of uncertainty and financial worry. News of thousands of deaths per day around the world because of the coronavirus filled our newsfeeds. Even though the disease reached our shores, it didn't have nearly the impact of poor old Italy, Spain or the USA.

The first subspecies of Crisis Kiwi that came to the forefront in this trying time was the Rumour-mill Kiwi. They always know someone who knows someone who knew someone who worked in politics. They had it on very good authority that the quarantine lockdown was coming: 'Just you watch, Cindy will do an address to the nation, and we'll all be self-isolating in our homes. Just you watch. Just you watch.'

And you would watch and there'd be no talk of quarantine (just yet).

The second subspecies of Crisis Kiwi to reveal themselves were the Panic Buyer Kiwis. Rumours, memes and one or two videos came from overseas showing foreigners desperately buying up all the toilet paper. I can only surmise that this kick-started New Zealand's own toilet-paper frenzy.

In the lead-up to the lockdown, I watched two yelling matches take place in the supermarket. First, a woman was chastising another woman for taking the last remaining four-pack of loo paper when she already had five other packs. Then a gentleman got very heated with a staff member over the vagueness around the next delivery of said paper. There were seven other people floating around, each with a slightly desperate look in their eye. But, I'm sure, if we all sat down and really questioned why we were so passionate about toilet paper, we would have realised it was the least of our worries. After all, we could always use pages from the Gideon Bibles we'd nicked from hotel rooms. We'd all just got caught up in the frenzy, thinking we must be missing something. If everyone else was buying toilet paper, obviously we had to as well!

After the toilet-paper shelves were emptied, the Panic Buyers went after the flour. A week into the lockdown, everyone was sharing photos on social media of the bread they had baked. Then came the banana bread, for some reason. A lot of banana bread. Then a whole wave of memes and tweets rose up, mocking those of us who had made the bread and the banana bread.

When the lockdown came and everyone was stuck in their houses, some Kiwis took it all very, very seriously. Others were more laissez-faire. A woman on our street made her way all along the footpath, chatting with whoever was in their garage or yard, leaning over fences as she went, having a whole lot of good-old gossipy chinwags. Oh, she just loved talking about our collective given circumstances and didn't care much for the enforced 'two-metre rule' designed to lessen the chance of infection.

On the flipside of that was the elderly woman who lived on the same street as my friend. She was at her window, practically 24/7, ringing up the cops if she saw absolutely anything that did not fit within the lockdown rules. Two neighbours talking too close – call the cops. Someone patting a stranger's dog – call the cops. She just loved the power she finally had.

The next subspecies to appear was the wonderful Conspiracy Theorists. I found myself spending too much time going onto strangers' Facebook pages and delving deep into their neuroses. The pandemic was manmade, they'd say. It was definitely manmade ... by the Chinese, of course. First, to take out the West, and second, to wipe out the baby boomer generation.

Then these Conspiracy Theorists joined forces with the Animal Rights Activists. Why did the Chinese have to eat bats?

Then it transformed into being about 5G, the latest generation of wireless communication technologies. Somehow that was the cause of the coronavirus. How? I'm not sure, but these guys' (and occasional girls') adamance had me questioning everything. They were so certain in their language that I even started thinking it was connected with JFK's assassination and the Loch Ness Monster.

During this time, there was a lot of shouting at each other on social media. People would show off about how productive they were being during lockdown, learning how to quilt and learning te reo ... at the same time. Then someone else would shout at them that they were bullying everyone into feeling like they had to be productive – and that that wasn't good for people's mental health.

There was a lot of talk about mental health during this time and a lot of posts about it being okay to just watch Netflix all day – you shouldn't feel like you have to be productive!

There was also a lot of people shouting that Jacinda was doing the best job, that she is basically a saint sent to save us. Others would then shout that she would be fired soon, then they'd detail how badly she was doing.

Artists would be shouting online about how, during the lockdown, you turn to books, Netflix, and music to get through, so don't you *ever* question the importance of artists! I'm not sure, however, if anyone was questioning that.

I guess the whole affair put people on edge, so they were instantly on the defensive.

But then there was the beautiful side of us banding together. Practically every house I passed on my daily walk around the block had a teddy bear in the window so children could do a teddy-bear hunt. Going to the supermarket, everyone kept their two-metre distance and shared smiles of encouragement and understanding. As I laboriously jogged through the park, which is very close to my house, I promise, I'd see families spending all their time together, as they walked and cycled whilst getting as much sun as they could. They all had this joy at being in each other's company. It was beautiful really.

CITY LIVING

Let's now head to the most heavily populated areas of this fair country, where various exquisite examples of humanhood hustle and bustle against each other in close proximity, where people pour in every morning full of reluctance, then eagerly leave when the day ends. I'm talking about our cities. They're where people work hard, party hard, fine dine, indulge in retail therapy, attend events and live the inner-city lifestyle. From shadowy downtown Auckland to frosty Invercargill's CBD, these urbane settings lure certain types of people, so let's meet them!

ROUGH SLEEPERS

In my opinion, there are three main categories of rough sleepers. There are the quiet, gentle kind you see sitting in the public library, keeping to themselves and not making a fuss. There are the chatty, squawky types who love having a conversation with you as much as they enjoy making loud noises to no one in particular on the other side of the street. Then there are the savvy lone wolves who cunningly survive out there on the streets.

A couple of years ago I was really hoodwinked as I was walking through Myers Park in central Auckland. This fellow walked up to me nursing his forearm, which was smeared with blood.

'Sorry, mate,' he said, clearly full of regret at having to approach me. 'I've just fallen off my bike. Is there any chance you've got some spare money for me to get a taxi to the hospital? I'm so sorry for having to ask you this. I hate asking for money, but I'm worried about my arm.'

'Oh my god. Of course!' I said. I only had a $10 note, but he assured me that would be fine. He promised to get the money back to me then strode off full of thanks. I was left wondering how exactly he planned to get that money back to me, but I quickly let it go.

Cut to two months later and I'm walking through Myers Park when the same fellow hurries up to me, nursing his forearm, which was streaked with blood.

'Sorry, mate,' he says, clearly full of regret at having to approach me. 'I've just fallen off my bike. Is there any chance you've got some spare money for me to get a taxi to the hospital? I'm so sorry for having to ask you this. I hate asking for money, but I'm worried about my arm.'

I wasn't as much of a sucker this time. I told him I didn't have any money. He told me that was fine, then ran up to the next park walker, who gave him $4.

The next time I was in Myers Park I saw him seated on a grassy knoll, basking in the sunshine and drinking an L&P. Beside him was a mound of musty, grimy bags. He seemed to be enjoying himself. I appreciate that a man's gotta do what a man's gotta do. He was clearly hoodwinking park walkers with fake blood because L&P doesn't pay for itself.

A while later, I started helping at the City Mission every Wednesday for an hour. I did this for a month before I came up with an excuse to miss a week then I just let it all go and never returned. I still carry guilt about that to this day.

Anyway, during that month I met a rough sleeper we'll call Poison. I'd seen him around the city a few times and knew he liked to sleep beneath the bridge in Arch Hill. If I were a rough sleeper, I think I would choose somewhere similar. It was always dry, free from wind, and the concrete bridge stored heat from the day and released it at night. Also, you could pretend to be a troll.

Poison had incredible watery eyes you could just fall into. He was also the quietest of the bunch. Let me tell you, there were some real characters who came into that mission, including a balding man who developed a crush on me. Somehow, he managed to get my phone number and sent me illicit text messages. Let's call him Simon.

I was intrigued by Poison and wanted to get to the bottom of his 'tragedy'. I sat beside him in the TV room and tried to strike up conversation by discussing the weather. He took a while to warm up to the conversation, but then told me about sleeping beneath the bridge and a little bit about his daily life.

Here I was assuming he was a depressed victim of the system, but he appeared to be quite happy with his life. He had a wife down south. He also had two daughters. He saw them whenever he was passing through. They were teenagers now. I wondered if they, too, were homeless. But it sounded like they had a wonderful home and went to school, where they studied hard.

Poison also had a brother up north whom he would see whenever he was passing through there. This brother was a successful fisherman with his own boat. So it wasn't like Poison didn't have people he could live with. He just didn't want to. A flat had even been organised for him to live in, but he couldn't handle the responsibility that came with having a home, so he abandoned it and resumed sleeping under the bridge.

It was about now in the conversation that Simon sidled up to me and asked me out on a date. I skirted around the question before sneaking away whilst he was distracted.

Years later, I was standing outside Auckland's Central City Library waiting to attend a fashion show inside. Don't ask me why but the fashion haus thought it was intriguing to have models walking amongst the bookshelves. But, to be honest, it turned out to be a brilliant show.

I'd only been given a solo ticket, so was standing all by myself in the queue looking my frumpy best, suddenly feeling intimidated by all the beautiful people around me. Then who should sidle up but Simon. He told me he slept in the cardboard city set up against the abandoned building across the road. I looked over and saw a rough-sleeping male and female having a shouting match whilst another man moved his sleeping bag into a new corner of the cardboard.

I then considered Simon. The doors to the library weren't opening any time soon. I was absolutely trapped. Simon decided to chew my ear off asking me about my love life and my sex life. Then he started talking about his mother, who lived in a suburban home across the bridge on the North Shore, and all the television he watched (which begs the question – where does he watch all this television if he lives in cardboard city?). It seemed he watched everything made in New Zealand. He was a walking encyclopaedia on the topic. Suddenly I felt more of a connection with this strange fellow than any of the beautiful people around us. But then Simon asked me what my cellphone number was so we could stay in touch. He said he'd texted me a while ago, but he never got a reply. I acted like I hadn't received the texts.

He took out his phone to put my number in (which begs the question – where does he charge his phone if he lives in cardboard city?). I gave him my number but changed the last digit. He said he'd text me right now so that I had his number.

'Get your phone out,' he said.

Thankfully, just then the doors to the library opened. In the cacophony I managed to avoid getting out my phone and simply gave him a friendly wave as I disappeared inside.

THE YUMMY MUMMY

A Yummy Mummy is an attractive, stylish young mother, usually in her twenties. Apparently, if you're an attractive and stylish mother later in life, you're a MILF. If you're an aggressively sexual MILF, you might be considered a Cougar.

In my mind there are two subsets of Yummy Mummies. There are those who fulfil the criteria but don't care/don't try/don't even know what a Yummy Mummy is. Then there are those who fully embrace the moniker and have it as part of their personal brand.

Of the former group, I noticed three attending my inner-city gym back in that long-forgotten time when I was a regular gym goer. They weren't friends but were all pregnant at the same time, seemingly due to give birth at the same time. They also all quickly resumed gym workouts within what seemed like days of having their babies. I'd see them in the group exercise room with a huge belly one week then washboard abs the next. (This was a gym in downtown Auckland, which had exercise classes that essentially replicated nightclub dancing at 9 am on a Sunday morning ... and all the clients were frothing for it.)

All three Yummy Mummies wore the latest skin-tight gym gear and had luscious long hair they would tie up into a ponytail. That ponytail would then be slotted through the hole at the back of their cap. They would all wear their caps down low over their eyes as if to hide their stunning beauty. They were feminine but, boy, were they strong. They lifted weights I couldn't even dream about and kicked the shit out of the boxing bags as their luscious ponytails whipped every which way.

Gyms naturally exude sexual pungency with hot people wearing very little whilst sweating and pumping pheromones into the air. But these women managed to get the most attention, even when they were nearly nine months pregnant (and still working out).

After pregnancy, they would come in and be holding their babies at reception, and men – and women, let's face it – would walk past and their eyes would just be drawn to their forms. On a biological, evolutionary level surely a woman would be less appealing with someone else's newborn baby on her hip, but somehow these women managed to override that. Perhaps the flush of motherhood in them just tipped us all over the edge.

These beautiful women's effortlessness can enrage some people, whilst plunging others into total self-loathing despair. I had a friend who gave birth and couldn't leave the house for two months. After that, she only managed to do one thing a day, whether it be go to the supermarket, take the baby to the doctor or even check the mailbox. As her mental health spiralled downwards, she decided exercise might help, so she forced me to force her to go to said inner-city gym.

I picked her up for our first workout together. Her skin was pale, bordering on grey, her hair was greasy, and her stomach was still flummery. As we walked into the gym, we passed a Yummy Mummy at reception having just collected her baby from the creche.

My friend asked, 'Is that her child?'

I nodded.

'Oh, fuck off,' my friend said, shaking her head before punishing herself on the treadmill.

She was so sleep-deprived she later walked into the men's changing rooms, used the toilet, walked past several confused, half-naked men and only realised what had happened as she mounted an exercycle.

On the flipside are the Yummy Mummies who think of, and refer to themselves as, Yummy Mummies. They usually have a big social media presence, and feature their children in every photo.

I follow one particular Kiwi Yummy Mummy, who regularly films herself in her car, having escaped her children in the house. She is always immaculately made-up, even though she makes out her videos are all off-the-cuff. She complains about her children, referencing their nastiest behaviours. She never softens her statements with 'but I love them, of course I love them'. No, she clearly hates her children.

I've watched these videos in minute detail. My favourite parts are when she gets distracted by her reflection in the rear-view mirror. There'll just be a microsecond of her either making sure she still looks immaculate, or suddenly being reminded of how beautiful she is. This is followed by a microsecond of her trying to find her train of thought before she plunges into how much she hates her kids again.

Don't get me wrong, she does display moments of loving her kids. These usually involve her, her husband and her children all wearing designer clothes in photos that one can only assume have gone through several draft versions before reaching the perfect one.

This heroine's life is also heavily consumerist. She often shows us what she is wearing today, sometimes displaying many newly bought outfits and asking us to comment with our favourite. She regularly talks about make-up and the latest food and diet crazes. I should point out that I don't think companies are paying her to do this publicity for them. I can't imagine them seeing much point as, surely, it's only me and a few women (who want to hate themselves) who are watching all her content.

I showed some of her videos to my grey-faced friend who'd joined me at the inner-city gym. She'd had three hours' sleep the night before and had developed mastitis. She and her partner were also on a budget as they were looking to buy a house, so all her baby's clothes were hand-me-downs from her sister-in-law. With an expressionless face, she watched a video of the Yummy Mummy and her daughter getting manicures. As soon as it ended, she simply said, 'Oh, fuck off!'

SOCIAL MEDIA KIWIS

Talking of social media … it's a relatively new phenomenon but, in my opinion, nothing has shaped us more as a nation and as a species than these pesky websites and photo-sharing platforms. In face-to-face contact, most Kiwis are reserved. They usually don't express what they are feeling, talk about how they're suffering, or share their inner-most thoughts. But chuck them onto a social media site and they are as honest and candid as possible, sharing insights into their mental illness or their vile hatred of someone or something, or waxing lyrical about their day as if it was so fascinating that everyone wants to know about it. In short, people are exposing their true nature to an invisible audience and I can't get enough of it.

There are those who are curating their lives. You've seen them at the drive-through at 2 am wildly sobbing as they order three cheeseburger combos and eat them all in quick succession in the carpark. The next day, you'll see them post a photo of themselves being beautifully charming and talking about motivation with their biceps out at the gym.

It's all so fascinating, and for someone who loves people-watching, I can do it all from the safety of my own dark little bedroom. What could be better?

There are two particular breeds of Social Media Kiwis I want to discuss in detail. First, there's the Blatant Narcissist who thinly disguises their narcissism through social warrior quotes or statements, but who leaves us all thinking, 'Why don't you just own the fact that you are a narcissist and that you love yourself. I think people would appreciate that more.'

There is one woman in my online sphere who tests a lot of people's patience. This woman would love to be described as 'fierce' and fancies herself as a staunch woman who 'takes no bullshit'. The pictures she posts of herself are, first and foremost, the most flattering she can take. I presume there are many taken before she's happy with the one she chooses to post. She's attractive in them, but also has a standoffish air about her. She is never smiling in the photos, and sometimes her lip is even curled with disdain. Beneath each photo will be a caption along the lines of: 'Do guys seriously think we'll pick up their clothes after them? Over this bullshit.'

Her friends/followers will comment with 'Preach, sister!' or 'Mic. Drop', but the comments she'll love the most are those that say things like 'Beautiful lady' or 'Absolute stunner'.

One photo is of her posing in the mirror, showing the side of her butt with a standoffish yet beautiful face. She's flipping the bird and the caption reads: 'Sick to death of the patriarchy. This bitch be tearing it down.'

All her friends/followers are there saying, 'Sing it, sister!', 'Punch patriarchy in the dick,' 'Stunning woman!' or 'Frothing over this pic, you are one stunning lady.'

Is she really tearing down the patriarchy with that photo? There are certainly issues with the patriarchy, and social media can be an effective instrument to help bring about social change and challenge people about their ingrained belief systems. But is this heroine really concerned with social change? Or is she maybe more interested in other things, like, say, admiration? I don't know ... I don't want to cast aspersions.

This breed of person also really loves when a social trend comes into play. We've lived through the 'Wear a hijab day' in support of New Zealand's Muslim community and the 'no make-up selfie'. Both are *very* righteous social causes, but I'm not sure if the people I'm talking about are really invested in these causes. They'll do a provocative pose whilst wearing a hijab and take the most flattering selfie possible without make-up on, then just lie back and wait for the 'Stunning lady' comments.

In saying all that, every time I meet this particular woman in person, she's great. She's polite and has a laugh, so ... I don't get it.

Talking about not really being invested in social causes, the other breed of Social Media Kiwis I love are called Virtue Signallers. Virtue signalling is publicly expressing opinions or sentiments intended to demonstrate your good character or the moral correctness of your position on a particular issue. These issues can be anything from mining in a rare dolphin's habitat to poor people sleeping in cars. I suspect Virtue Signallers don't actually believe in the opinions or sentiments they are spouting about on social media. Perhaps these Virtue Signallers only want other people to believe they believe in the opinions and sentiments because it makes them appear to be better people than they really are. Are you following me?

Let me give you an example. There's one man whose every social media post is … trying. He constantly posts articles or videos that express misogyny or homophobia or racism with a comment like 'This disgusts me.' It would seem he does this with the aim of showing off how great it is that he isn't misogynistic or homophobic or racist.

But I question if deep down he really cares about the issues. When Notre Dame in Paris burnt down and some very wealthy benefactors announced they would pour millions into rebuilding it, our hero, the Virtue Signaller, was quick to post: 'I find it disgusting that Paris has such a homeless people problem and yet millions are being poured into the Notre Dame rebuild. It's disgusting and we need to get our priorities right.'

He then posted a further six articles with comments like 'Absolutely disgusting' and 'This is what's wrong with the world'. Then all his friends/followers commented saying how right he was and how unjust the whole world is.

Next, he shared an online petition with the aim of stopping the billionaires pouring millions into Notre Dame, even though it's impossible to see how that would work.

Not long afterwards, I met him in the flesh and asked him how his campaigning was going around solving the homelessness crisis in Paris.

He looked at me with a frown. 'What are you talking about?'

'Oh, I just assumed with all your online campaigning that you're working hard to solve the homeless crisis that affects so many people.'

He blustered and shrugged it off then tried to get out of the conversation, so I pressed him on it. He said that posting about it on social media helped get the word out there and bring about change. (Because nothing will bring about social change in Paris quicker than a few Kiwis' Facebook friends signing a petition.)

I don't want to cast aspersions, but maybe he just likes the fact that we all *think* he cares about income inequality and helping those less fortunate than ourselves, but actually doing something to fix these problems isn't of much interest to him, or would take too much effort. I don't know. I don't want to cast aspersions. Winky face.

THE GAY POSSE

You see these groups a lot on social media. A row of photogenic young gay men, some of them doing fierce poses with their eyes slightly closed, their mouths slightly pouted. Others are smiling whilst surreptitiously flexing their biceps. If it's summertime, they are headed to the beach, or to Sydney for Mardi Gras, or they're spending New Years together.

They wear singlets with huge arm holes, allowing ample view of their ribs or the sides of their washboard abs. They also wear neat, clean shorts, maybe with the hem folded up, and a shoe with no sock or with tiny socks hidden beneath the rim of the shoe. These boys dress the same; there's definitely a pack mentality going on.

Their faces are most likely well-groomed. If there is facial hair, it'll be a closely cropped beard. Ungainly stubble is unheard of. Highly manicured stubble is acceptable. Eyebrows are always well kept and make-up (foundation) is common.

Some of the boys are more prone to athleticism than others. That doesn't stop those with slower metabolisms, however, from hitting the gym hard for the two months leading up to whatever pride event they are attending.

If they *are* attending a pride event, the fancy dress aspect of it will always attract a specific costume. It will be a thin, strappy harness that goes around the shoulders. This will be teamed with matching hotpants. If there is a particular theme to the party, this harness/hotpants combo can be catered to it. Say the theme is 'Heaven and Hell' these boys may attach white-feathered wings to the harness and – voila! – you've got yourself a sexy angel. If you want to be a devil, simply wear devil horns with your harness and hotpants and – voila! – you've got yourself a sexy devil.

These packs of beautiful gay men are a fascinating phenomenon. Have they banded together as outsiders who rely on each other for support? Or are they more like the Cool Girls at high school? The catty and exclusive ones everyone wants to be friends with.

I'm fascinated by this species. There is always a particular member of the Gay Posse who I find most interesting. This individual is invariably less attractive than everyone else in the group. They are invariably less likely to score or have a boyfriend. They adore being part of the cool group but are constantly on edge because their social standing is fleeting, and they worry they'll soon be left by the wayside.

I've observed a few of these types of boys but have only analysed one close up. Let's call him Adrian. I attended a party and the whole posse was there. They were a clique of attractive gay men whose facial expressions and demeanours could never be described as 'welcoming' – and then there was Adrian out on the back deck, smoking.

When I first saw him, he was screeching about something to a small audience. As I gravitated towards him, I heard him use common drag parlance: 'Yas queen!' and 'Oh henny'. When someone said something he agreed with, Adrian would enthusiastically click his fingers as a way of communicating that agreeance.

He was neither muscular like half of the posse, nor skeletally thin like the other half. He was definitely soft around the edges. He was wearing ballooning pants, which tapered down to the ankle, where he worked high heels. He wore a 1980s women's jacket and mascara and he had one dangling earring that ended with a feather. His nails were painted in intricate designs, which couldn't quite draw attention away from the fact he chewed them. He had glasses and short-cropped blonde hair.

Later that night, I ended up at the same table as Adrian. What eventuated was a one-sided conversation. I would ask him questions, and he would answer at a mile a minute, then he would ask me nothing in return.

I found out he worked at the council and he was 'fucking good' at his job apparently. He feigned annoyance at having to work and feigned annoyance that everyone thought he was so 'fucking good' at it. Apparently one of his co-workers was surprised he was given a promotion, after only six months of being there, to which Adrian replied, 'Of course I should be promoted because I'm fucking good at my job!'

What did his actual job entail? Organising events, I think. Apparently he'd had people try to headhunt him several times but he'd turned them all down.

After 20 minutes, during which he hadn't found out a single thing about me, he started looking across the rest of the room to see who was there. His stubbed out his eighth cigarette of the evening, made his excuses, then hurried over to a new arrival, who had shown up in full, fantastic drag. Adrian then hovered around the outside of the group until he found an opportunity to step forward and scream about how fierce the henny drag queen was looking.

Later in the evening, he excused himself to go to the bathroom. On returning to the living room, he found his friends had all bunched together for a photo. He lurked around awkwardly until one of them told him to get into the photo. He clapped his hands and ran around the back of the group where he had to stand on tiptoes in order to be seen in the shot.

The night drew on and everyone ventured to a gay bar in the grungiest part of the inner city. I invited myself along for the social experiment. Adrian loved screaming all the lyrics of the songs playing on the dancefloor. Eventually, though, he found himself abandoned. The rest of his posse were either hooking up with each other in various shady corners or had drifted away without a second thought for him.

I found him standing by the bar nursing a vodka soda. He was very happy for my company. He complained that he had to go to work on Monday because he was organising an event that he couldn't entrust to anyone else because no one was as 'fucking good' as he was.

At one point, the rest of his attractive Gay Posse congregated to plan what to do next. Adrian was 'easy' to just do whatever everyone else wanted, but no one heard him make this proclamation. Eventually, everyone decided to part ways for the evening. The last I saw of Adrian was him getting into an Uber by himself and disappearing down the street. He was probably heading home to think through the 'fucking amazing' event he was planning.

RELIGIOUS ZEALOTS

When it comes to religious types there are the subtle ones, who wear a little cross around their neck that you think nothing of. That is until two months into your friendship when they lightly drop something like, 'God's always listening if you need an ear, buddy.'

Then there are the Zealots – the religious types who loudly and proudly broadcast their beliefs to the world, and the ones who choose to advance their agenda more insidiously.

As a late teen, freshly moved to Auckland, I was approached by a very tall woman in a tweed pant-suit on Queen Street. She asked me if I'd like to do a personality test.

Having a fleeting bout of narcissism, I was excited to find out more about myself, so I readily followed her into a nearby building, where we went up in the elevator without any conversation. There, I did her personality test and she showed me the resulting graph. It made no sense to me, but, apparently, I was failing in various aspects of my personality. She suggested I buy a very big/expensive book on Dianetics. Unfortunately (slash fortunately) I was a very poor student so couldn't fork out the cash and left empty-handed.

It wasn't until years later I realised I'd had my first brush with Scientology that day.

Then there are the Hare Krishnas, who float around the various main streets of New Zealand cities. Their energy is universally odd. Every single one of them looks at you unlike any other human would. There's an intensity there as they ask you various questions. When you respond with a joke, there is no reaction – just a blank face with a serene half-smile.

And, of course, there's the wonderful Jehovah's Witnesses that come a-knocking, handing over their booklets showing lions sitting with lambs beneath a rainbow and a group of people of the most diverse cultures in their traditional garb smiling out at you.

During my childhood, the Jehovah's Witnesses were the most vilified subsection of society. Other kids would share hilarious stories about how their fathers got out their shotguns and told the door-knocking Jehovah's Witnesses to piss off whenever they approached. And we'd all laugh.

When the religious instruction teacher would come to school with colouring books and the promise of a doughnut if we coloured Noah's boat in the best, the two Jehovah's Witness kids in our class would be put into a separate room. I felt sorry that they didn't have the chance of winning a doughnut, but I also thought they were weird. I also felt sorry for them because their parents' religious decisions instantly set them apart. I had all these thoughts without ever questioning the fact that my parents had agreed to me taking religious studies classes with Mr Connelly.

For years, there was one man who stood on the corner of Queen and Victoria streets in central Auckland late on Friday and Saturday nights. He held a well-thumbed Bible in his palm, and he would hold it up, the gold cross embossed onto the leather binding shining in the streetlight. People completely ignored him, and he completely ignored them as a diatribe of words poured from his mouth.

For months, I barely noticed him. I was aware of his presence and had rolled my eyes with my friends, assuming him to be a complete bigot. Eventually, I decided not to jump to conclusions and to listen to what he was saying. Perhaps he was preaching love and world peace … Alas, I soon found out he was saying we'd all be subjected to eternal damnation for the way we were conducting our lives.

The fact he wasn't connecting with anyone really intrigued me. He refused to make eye contact, and his word vomit simply mixed in with the night-time sounds of buses braking, nightclubs pulsing and people yelling and screaming at each other.

One night, I sat on a park bench near this preacher, enjoying my late-night Burger King, having escaped from a painful social situation a few blocks away. After 20 minutes he finally made eye contact with me by accident, or maybe to make sure I wasn't a threat. I smiled and got in a quick 'How's it going?'

He looked shocked. I don't think anyone had ever tried to engage with him. He nodded in response.

'Good night for it,' I offered.

Maybe he thought I was a lost soul; he decided to break from his religious fervour to talk to me about Christ. I wasn't having it. I kept mining him for details about his own life. His name was Isileli. He was born in Tonga but had come here before he was one. His father was a preacher and he fell into step with his beliefs without much thought. He preached here on Friday and Saturday nights because it was the will of God. I presume he meant it was written somewhere in the Bible.

I asked if God spoke to him.

'Of course,' he replied.

'What does he sound like?'

'It's not a *voice* voice,' he told me.

I could have plunged into the hypocrisy of it all but decided to avoid that. What followed was a beautiful theological debate, which mined into the very reason for our existence.

We both came to the conclusion that if everyone was as devout a Christian as him, then life would be very boring as he would have nothing to rail against, and perhaps what makes life so wonderful is the huge spectrum of humanity from the sinniest of sinners to the purest of pures.

It was very late by the time we stopped chatting. He gave me a solid handshake with his big hands, and I went on my way. The next time I was in town, though, he was there again, his Bible held high to the sky as he avoided eye contact. When I passed by, my wave caught his eye and his eyes lit up for the briefest of moments.

ROAD RAGERS

One thing New Zealanders do well is road rage. Where better to do that than deep in our cities where there are a lot of cars?

By 'do well', what I mean is we're terrible at it. Is that a double negative? You know what I mean. If road rage was an Olympic sport, we'd be champions at it. Most of my foreign friends would agree with this. They've never seen anything quite like it.

It seems strange that we should have so much anger around driving. I've been in traffic in China and India, where people just pull out into the fast flow of traffic, where you are constantly almost killed, but it's all water off a duck's back. No one seems to have any ill will about it.

In my experience, road rage is expressed most often when someone is distracted at the lights. You're a little too slow reacting to the green light and suddenly the Road Rager behind you is honking their horn, screaming, 'Hurry the fuck up, you fucking fuckwit!'

Pull out into traffic just a little too late and the car coming towards you won't slow down until the last minute to 'teach you a lesson'. Then you feel them behind you as you pull up at a red traffic light. Fate is clearly against you as they pull up right beside you. You avoid eye contact, acting like you are in a daze, trying to curate your face into one of sweetness so they'll forgive you. But the lights are still red, and you quickly chance a look over at the other driver. They are indeed looking at you. They're either shaking their head very slowly and menacingly, or they're red-faced and screaming profanities at you. Somehow, you've triggered something deep inside them even though – as well as being a Road Rager – they're just some suburban mum heading home after a day at work, or they're a lovely dad who adores his two daughters.

Finally, the lights change to green. You hover back so that your new mate can drive off and leave you alone. You drive into the intersection but you're not paying attention and traffic is very heavy. Suddenly you find yourself hovering in the middle of the goddamn intersection. The lights go orange … and you're not moving. You're directly in line with the traffic coming the other way. The lights go red. You're still there, just trying to look ahead and be nonchalant about the whole thing. The other light goes green. The oncoming traffic ferociously honk their horns at you as they have to indicate and manoeuvre around you, or simply wait through a whole cycle of lights until you can finally move forward. I have been in that situation far too often.

That said, I can road rage with the best of them. God, heavy traffic infuriates me. I can be in my car screaming at everyone to 'Hurry the fuck up, would you? Can you please just fucking move! *Move!*', even though it's invariably my fault for not factoring in the fact it takes more than five minutes to drive across town.

I'm blessed that I rarely need to travel during rush hour. At one stage, however, I had an evening job out in the eastern suburbs of Auckland. Google Maps would usually say it would take 30 minutes to arrive at my destination, but during rush hour it leapt up to an hour and a half. I had to take that route every day for 10 days. On the first day, we were crawling along, like, I was lucky if I got to five k an hour. Amid pointless screams at the cars in front of me, I started to think, 'Surely it can't be this bad. Something must've happened.'

Half an hour later, I could see there had been an 'incident' on the road in front of me and the traffic had been directed into two lanes. Once through that bottleneck, traffic was flowing, so I breathed a sigh of relief ... until I reached the incident.

Two cars were completely smooshed into each other. Glass and oil were smattered across the tarseal. Multiple police cars were parked around, and an ambulance was parked nearby. Two people on stretchers were being wheeled into the back of the ambulance. It was brutal but, once I was through the bottleneck, I pretty much forgot about it.

The next day the traffic was bumper-to-bumper even earlier into my commute. After screaming at the traffic, I thought, 'This can't be right.' Lo and behold, another car crash and more people being taken off by ambulance.

In total, over the 10 nights I did that trip, there were accidents on nine of them, six of which required ambulances. Each time, though, once I was through the annoyance of the bottleneck, I clean forgot about them.

As I was driving home on the last night of that job, I suddenly realised everyone buys into the lottery of rush-hour traffic. Every day we all take the gamble – will this be the time that we are the ambulance-inducing accident waiting to happen? Will we live to see another day?

Can I just end with my own personal bugbear with the whole traffic thing? It's pedestrian-only traffic lights in the middle of the street, the ones that only go red when a pedestrian pushes the button when they want to cross. Well, what I find usually happens in this scenario is that the walker or runner reaches the traffic light and pushes the button. They then see no traffic is coming and safely cross. Meanwhile, you're racing down the road, late (by your own doing) for some sort of appointment when suddenly you have to stop at these lights – for *no one*. Then you just sit there like a chump, staring ahead, wishing for the day they hurry up and make hover cars already.

THE QUESTION TIME WANKER

Okay, so if you've ever attended any sort of seminar, or lecture, or community talk, you'll have come across a Question Time Wanker. They are most prevalent when an internationally famous person, or one of our own who has had huge success, comes to give a talk at a huge venue in the city centre.

Let's say this famous person is David Attenborough or Margaret Atwood. (Actually, let's not include them. I'm worried they'll be dead by the time this is published. And if they're not, let's get prepared for it because it's going to happen, and we have to be ready.) Instead, let's say it's Steven Spielberg.

The great director has deigned to come to New Zealand to share his experiences with an audience of 2000 people in a theatre downtown. This man is a genius and his time is precious, people.

We have all sat through a scintillating hour, run by an excellent interviewer, and we are all feeling loved-up towards Steven. Then the interviewer turns to the audience and says, 'Okay, we're going to open up to the audience for question time. Remember we only have five minutes, so try to keep the questions short.'

A guy takes the microphone from a young usher, who is running around whilst trying to keep out of everyone's sightline, and our new mate – let's call him Adam – begins.

'First of all, Steven, welcome to New Zealand. Tena koutou. We really appreciate you being here. I think I speak for us all when I say I hope you've had a chance to appreciate what our beautiful country has to offer.'

Okay, so first off, that took too long. The interviewer said they only have five minutes.

'Second of all, Steven,' Adam continues, 'I just want to thank you for being the artist of our times, creating the cinematic landscape for our lifetime.'

At this point, you can feel the rest of the audience deflate, but it looks like he's getting to his question.

'I guess my question is ...' Then he pauses to think about how to word it. YOU KNEW QUESTION TIME WAS COMING. PREP YOUR QUESTION!

'I guess I preface my question with the fact that I'm working on my own screenplays at the moment.'

At this point, there would be a collective groan if the audience wasn't so damn polite. Instead, most of us are thinking, 'Oh, here we fucking go ...'

'I feel the screenplays are at a really good place. I'm getting a lot of buzz around them, especially in my writers' group. One of them is, actually you'll get a real kick out of this ...' Adam laughs pre-emptively and has a sideways smirk like he's being a bit cheeky. 'It's actually a light-hearted kids' alien movie. Kinda inspired by *E.T.* if I'm honest. But I promise it's not. It's an improvement on *E.T.*'

Everyone tenses at the slight. Steven Spielberg doesn't seem to register it, though. Maybe he's having trouble understanding Adam's Kiwi accent ...

At this point, the young usher is hovering close to Adam, her hand ready to yank the microphone at any point. She knows she's going to get reprimanded for this, but she's too polite to just take it.

'And the other one,' Adam continues, 'is actually a war-time movie following some young Kiwi men heading off to Gallipoli and just the kinda brutal rigmarole all that was. Some guys were so young. Too young. It's incredible what they went through ...' He shakes his head as if lost in thought then restarts: 'I actually had to do a lot of research for that one.'

By now, the audience are screaming silently inside their heads: 'Shut the fuck up!'

'So yeah ...' Adam says casually, then suddenly remembers that this is question time and he's supposed to ask a question even though he'd really just stood up to brag and have some camaraderie with Steven Spielberg. His brain desperately scans for something to ask. 'So, I guess my question is what would you do with them now, now that you've got your scripts into a place that you're really happy with?'

The usher hovers her hand towards the questioner, signalling to Adam to give the microphone back. He is oblivious to her, gripping the microphone to his chest. He seems to think there's going to be some friendly back-and-forth with Steven.

'Well, big question,' Spielberg says, and everyone laughs because that's what you do. But no one actually, deep down in their funny bone, found that statement funny. 'They actually sound like really good script ideas,' he says. 'Maybe we could talk after the session?'

The interviewer then tells everyone the five-minute question time is up. There is a big round of applause for Steven Spielberg. Adam hurries up on stage as everyone files out, and he and Steven seem to have a great conversation.

The interviewer then ushers them both offstage into the wings of the theatre where they have a beer together. Steven buys the rights to both screenplays that night, then he directs them both and they are both Oscar winners. Adam buys a house in LA and is suddenly the talk of the town.

Two years later, he is giving a talk to an audience of 2000 people – and I'm sitting in the audience watching him from row AA (because rows A to Z were already booked out because he is so beloved by the nation).

He shares some candid stories about all the amazing people he's met and worked with, and he warrants genuine laughs from people. This is not forced laughter because he is so charming.

Meanwhile, the screenplay I've been working on since well before Steven Spielberg visited has stagnated and nobody is interested in it. I sit there wondering why I don't have the confidence – gaul – to take that microphone and brag about my own project. I'll tell you why. It's because I'm not an absolute wanker.

WEIGHT-CONSCIOUS KIWIS

Obviously being overweight, and the health complications that come with that, are of serious concern in New Zealand. And I feel it, man. Losing weight is so hard! I'm living the nightmare – but I've always assumed it wasn't something you really talked about. You know, we don't like talking about our issues.

But then I landed a most wonderful job, working at a television production company in the city centre. It was on a weight-loss TV show. I can't even remember what it was called but it followed various New Zealanders on their weight-loss journeys. My job was to watch all the footage from each day's filming. I then had to write out and time-code every line of dialogue from the participants. At least, I think it's called time-coding.

I got to be the ultimate voyeur. The people being filmed had no idea I was watching them expose their deepest and darkest secrets. Sick, right? But also amazing. It was hard work, though, and I was eventually fired because I was too slow at it. I partially blame becoming so invested in one couple's story that I forgot to write down what they said.

The wife, a wonderfully frumpy sort of person, took on the catchphrase 'I'm bringing sexy back', and would mutter it every time she began a workout. Her husband was a workaholic who would only consume coffee during the day. At night, though, he'd eat a full pizza then two litres of ice cream.

I felt for these guys because they were working so much that the last thing they wanted when they got home was a low-joule spinach smoothie. Sometimes a big cheesy pizza was the only highlight of their day. I get it.

It turned out, however, that the husband only had a weight problem because there was a benign tumour pressing onto a certain part of his brain. He started taking medication to stop the effects of the tumour and promptly lost all the weight – without making any effort.

His poor humourless wife had started out with a husband to share all the highs and lows of weight loss with, but now she was on the journey all by herself. Her husband simply kicked back and enjoyed his macaroni cheese. His wife's resentment and disappointment were palpable. And here I was watching all their unguarded emotions in the raw footage.

As their relationship began to unravel, I felt it was mostly his fault. When, for example, she told him she'd had a bad day and had somehow managed to put on a kilo despite working so hard on her diet, he shrugged and suggested she needed to try harder.

The producer of the TV show was a real character as well. And she definitely fell into this subspecies of New Zealander. She was quite rotund and was always puffing by the time she reached the top of the stairs of the two-storey building. She always wore black, a very slimming colour. She also spent a lot of money on her hair, nails and skin. Her black hair was slick and incredible. Her nails were always perfectly manicured, and her spray tan made her look like she had always just come back from Club Med. But I sensed all this beautifying was a band-aid on her real issue.

She wasn't a pleasant woman to be around and could be quite horrid to people. I mused that if she were a little healthier, maybe she'd be less impatient with everyone who came into her sphere of existence.

I remember her wheezing up the stairs to the edit suite as I was handing over my time-coding. The editors were working on the episode of my couple and, as she collapsed into her chair, she said, 'What are the fat bastards up to now?' without any sense of irony or self-awareness.

I often wonder what happened to my overweight TV couple, seeing as I was fired and didn't manage to see out their story. I know the wife managed to lose seven kilos over the time I was following her, and she definitely managed to get some degree of 'sexy back'. I couldn't help but be proud of her.

On the flipside, I have been around a fair few people who are constantly on diets or are struggling with some sort of eating disorder. I lived with one woman who would record her exercising down to the minute.

'Okay,' she'd say, 'so I walked for thirty-seven minutes this morning, and I'll take another twenty-two minutes to walk to the gym, so I only have one hour and one minute to reach my daily quota of two hours.'

She'd tell me this without any awareness of how … extreme she sounded. She would often also share with me how much protein she'd eaten in a day. 'I had three hundred grams of salmon today. I feel like a fat bitch.'

She knew the nutritional value of everything and once told me I'd have to run the length of a rugby field five times to burn off just one M&M.

All her good work was occasionally undercut by a binge. The poor woman was plagued by food. I could hear her scurrying into the kitchen at night to make bowl after bowl of muesli. I'd also occasionally wake up to find a Post-it note saying that she'd eaten something of mine and she'd replace it as soon as she was paid.

Eventually, we drifted apart, but years later I would see her pounding the pavement, walking with some vigour, her face drawn and haunted.

I'd love to quickly take the opportunity to point out a couple of other amazing Weight-Conscious Kiwis. There's the dieter who is on a points-based system. They can't help but share with you how many points your meal is. 'That Trumpet ice cream is over half your point allocation!'

'But I'm not on your points-system diet!' I'd cry in response.

Then there's the no-carbohydrates dieter. I worked in close proximity with one. His body was great, sure, but he was constantly in ketosis. If you got within a metre radius of his being, there was a chance you'd pass out from his halitosis. Poor guy – poor, attractive, guy.

HOROSCOPE HONEYS

We all know people who make important decisions based on the zodiac: 'Well, he was a Leo and I was a Taurus, and we just aren't meant to be together, so we got divorced.' Then there are the ones who write people off because of when they were born: 'I just didn't get a good vibe from her. Turns out she was a Scorpio, so that explains everything. She had a real sting in her tail.' One of my favourite lines is: 'You're an Aquarius, are you? Ah, that makes a lot of sense.' Does it? Does it really, Kristin?

Unfortunately, when I meet Horoscope Honeys, I always forget to test their zodiac prowess by challenging them to guess my star sign. Instead, I willingly give up that information only to be met with: 'Ah yes, I was going to say I knew you were an Aquarius. That makes a lot of sense.'

Then there's the next-level astrology lovers. They are desperate to 'do your numbers' and get you to call up your mother to find out what time of day you were born. Let me tell you, I got caught up in the frenzy with one of them and was beyond livid that my mother couldn't recall what time of day I was born.

'Well, do you have a vague idea?'

'I'm pretty sure it was at night.'

'That's not good enough, Mum. I need the hour. I need the minute. I need the second that I came into this goddamn world. Otherwise, how am I going to know about all the things that are rising. Your Venuses, or your Uranuses, or what have you?!'

In short, there is a subspecies of New Zealanders who have bought into the zodiac wholeheartedly. They all seem to have a degree of intelligence and I'm sure, if you pressed them, if you got deep down into the recesses of their truth, that they would tell you it's all BS. But, for the most part, they want people to think they believe it.

In saying all that, I guess it is quite fun. It's another way to categorise people. Hell, maybe I should rethink this book and just do a zodiac personality book instead …

At a party in downtown Christchurch a few years ago, I met a seemingly well-put-together woman. With jet-black hair held up with a zany headscarf, she was beautiful. She'd been born in Hong Kong and she definitely had a sophisticated, international air about her. Let's call her Julia.

The most attractive quality about her was her husky voice. She had a perfect voice for radio, but I reckon, in hindsight, that her true calling was being on a zodiac hotline – if such things still exist. I could imagine calling her up, telling her I was an Aquarius ('Ah yes, I was going to say that – I knew you were an Aquarius') then listening to her chocolatey voice tell me what I had in store for the next few weeks.

She took a keen interest in me and my partner at the time, who was a Cancer.

Her mouth tightened a little. 'And you're an Aquarius?'

'That's right.'

She nodded and closed her eyes a little. 'Do you want me to just lay it on you?'

'Lay what on me?'

'Cancers and Aquarians don't mesh. How long have you been together?'

'Eight years.'

'Oh boy.'

'Why?' I asked desperately. 'Why don't we mesh?'

'Cancers are homebodies. They want surety and things to go in a predictable way. Aquarians are the zany ones of the zodiac. They're all about breaking form and cutting loose and being zany.'

I nodded, never really having considered myself to be 'zany' but glad for the compliment.

Look, the relationship did end. I mean, it could've been that Julia had planted a terrible seed, or maybe she had enlightened me to the truth of the situation. He was a homebody and I was all about cutting loose and being zany. Or did I just begin to subscribe to that belief about myself because Julia had told me that's what I subscribed to? Oh look, I don't know.

During another trip to Christchurch, I visited Julia at her flat and she showed me a zodiac book that broke down every single day of the year. I raced to the page for 3 February and pored over it. There was some specific shit in there and I adhered to all of it. Yes, I do hate following the rules. Yes, I do vibe well with Librans. Yes, I do have back problems, specifically the lower spine. Yes, I do procrastinate and have problems with deadlines. Yes, I am 'zany'.

'How can that be, though?'

Julia shrugged as if to say, 'Some things the human mind simply can't comprehend.'

She gave me a palm reading as well, something she was getting into with gusto, and said she could see money in my future.

'Having it or not having it?' I asked.

'Exactly,' she replied.

I frowned but didn't press the issue.

'Are your parents still together?' Julia asked.

'Yes.'

'Oh,' she said, surprised. 'Okay, well, one of them is going to live until they're over one hundred. One of them will die pretty soon, I think.'

'Oh my god. Do you know which is which?'

'No,' she whispered. 'Do you know your Chinese sign?'

'Umm, dog?'

'Ah yes. That makes a lot of sense,' she said as she placed my hand gently back onto my lap and smiled knowingly at me.

I left that day stinking of incense and wondering if there was any such thing as free will, or whether everything was predetermined by the stars.

The following weekend I met someone who shared the same birthday as me – and we couldn't have been more different. He was very good at business, had no back problems and was most definitely not 'zany'. I discussed this with Julia next time I saw her, but she simply said, 'Yes, but what *time* of the day was he born?'

SMALL-TOWN FOLK

Driving from city to city, racing through small towns along the way, one might be tempted to ask: 'What do people actually do in this town? How do they spend their time? Why does this settlement actually even exist? What is it servicing?' These are good questions, but I don't have the answers to any of them. What I do know is, if you scratch the surface, you'll find a delightful array of characters living, breathing and being passionate about sometimes very eccentric things in these towns. Without further ado, let's meet some of New Zealand's small-town folk.

AM-DRAM COSTUME DESIGNERS

A big call, but amateur dramatic societies are the lifeblood of small-town New Zealand. They combine Kiwis of all ages with a common goal. There's the young high-school students and the older folk, there are those with aspirations of being professional actors and those that just get a buzz out of being on stage and giving it their all. At the heart of every amateur production is, of course, the Costume Designer.

Am-Dram Costume Designers come in three varieties. There's the middle-aged woman on the rounder side with a snazzy haircut (think a zany porcupine body in either a bold copper or with blonde/blackberry streaks). These women wear breezy, floaty numbers and love a scarf with a flourish.

Then there's the elderly lady with functional grey hair and modest lipstick. Sometimes they don't have much in the way of lips, but they put lipstick on anyway. This heroine wears sensible slacks and a comfortable shoe. She'll wear a turtleneck top with a sleeping-bag material vest over the top during the colder months.

Thirdly, there is the older, camp gay man. Usually of the more rotund persuasion, they have thinning, wayward hair and glasses perched on the end of their noses, through which they look at you – or down on you. They always have a measuring tape hanging around their neck, and they nearly always disagree with their director, but never vocally. The director will give their direction and our sassy costume designer will bite his tongue then mutter his grievances to the actor as they fix their hems.

This particular costume designer isn't afraid of 'going sexy' with his costumes. He'll accentuate any décolletage and tell the actresses that it's all 'teeth and tits'. He'll flirt with the young male lead, using sexual innuendo that goes over the actor's head.

All three subsets of the Am-Dram Costume Designer are whizzes on sewing machines and love holding pins between their lips, whether they need them there or not.

These three subspecies of lovelies are behind the scenes for every amateur production, from the Christmas-time pantomime of *Aladdin*, where a white woman plays the titular role, to the cutting-edge production of *Chess* with all its 1990s aesthetics, to one of Roger Hall's older plays, which completely sells out to a British farce involving a lot of miscommunication and opening doors.

Whatever the production, it's usually the 'last one I'll do', because it's a stressful job sewing 25 furry cat heads with ears for *The Alley Cats of Putaruru* (a knock-off of Andrew Lloyd Webber's *Cats*, which gets around the expensive production rights), and the work they do very rarely gets the kudos it deserves, and there are uppity actors taking exception to it – 'I don't want to be the tortoiseshell cat. I want to be the tabby!'.

In any case, the costume designer will get through that production and vow never to do it again. But then the director will ring them up, explaining that the new production of *No Sex Please, We're British* couldn't possibly happen without their expertise. And so, our heroes and heroines are yanked out of retirement and are back in the rehearsal room, measuring a young actress's waist and marvelling at how slim it is.

I should also make a note that all three types of costume designers secretly love a crisis but will always grumble about it. The director has had a change of heart and now wants all 25 cats' heads to be made of latex, and they're needed by Monday rehearsal. Our heroes and heroines will bitch and moan all weekend but deliver the cats' heads by Monday. When they're thanked profusely, they'll simply shrug as if to say, 'What did you expect? I'm talented.'

Of all the costumers I've worked with over the years, one who has stayed firmly in my mind worked on a Summer Shakespeare production of *Twelfth Night*. Let's call her Janet. I can't actually remember her name, but I think it probably was Janet. She was of the older persuasion, with a sensible haircut and lipstick on her no-lips.

The aesthetic the director was going for was pretty wacky. Plain jeans bedazzled with sequins and swirly designs made using puffy purple paint. The cast had to source our own jeans from a second-hand store, and we were then reimbursed. I made the mistake of getting women's jeans without realising it, so they were baggy around the hip and tapered at the knee but with a boot-cut flair. By the time I realised this, the sequins and purple swirls had been attached and I had to commit to them for our month-long season.

I had a small part in the show, playing the lead's twin brother, and I was absolutely terrible at it, mostly because of arrogance. How dare the director tell me to be louder and faster?

I wasn't the only one who was terrible. By production week, which is the final week of rehearsals before opening night, the whole production was falling apart at the seams. None of the untrained actors could be heard in the outdoor setting, nor did any of them understand the Shakespearean language pouring from their mouths. On top of that, it was a particularly wet summer, so performing outside was proving difficult. Added to that was a stagnant gutter of rainwater above the performance space, which bred countless mosquitoes that devoured us.

The poor director was understandably having a meltdown. In front of everyone, she ended up taking all her frustrations out on Janet before storming off. Janet took it all on the chin, her face remaining perfectly neutral throughout. The cast were at a loss. We just sat around wondering if the whole show was going to be called off.

Instead, Janet stepped up to the plate and took charge. She told us to get into position for the next run of the show. Afterwards she took me aside and told me I had to be faster and louder. She also explained that it was boring if actors took too long, and that if the audience couldn't hear me they would zone out. All of which made sense to me and I think I improved.

The director arrived back for the second run of the show and was startled by how much we had all improved. She looked lovingly/thankfully at Janet, who shrugged a shrug that read as, 'What did you expect? I'm talented.'

By opening night, we all thought we were a triumph, though in hindsight we were still terrible, me especially. But, boy, were we buzzing and so was Janet. She and the director got drunk on wine and danced together as if the wee spat had never taken place. Janet was the winner on the day. In saying that, the sequins started falling off three days into the season and were all but gone by week two, so she wasn't that good.

THE FLY HATER

There is a constant war going on in New Zealand, a war of which most of us are unaware – the war between geriatric New Zealanders and flies. These humans are usually 80+ and they always have a fly swat at the ready. Their sight is usually failing, but they can still spot a fly 20 metres away. Using reflexes that haven't been tested for decades, they are determined to kill that goddamn fly. Once it's squashed onto their swat, the Fly Hater will quietly scrape the carcass off onto the carpet, satisfied with their quarry.

A disproportionate amount of the Fly Hater's conversation revolves around flies and their destruction.

They are well informed on the latest fly spray and what conditions are necessary for a fly population explosion. When food is placed on a table, their hands constantly wave back and forth above it.

My grandmother was a great Fly Hater, renowned even, but the biggest Fly Hater I have ever met was a man we'll call Cecil, because Cecil is such a wonderful name for an old man.

I was 17 and, for some reason, had been peer-pressured into partaking in an odd scheme. It involved high-school students spending afternoons with elderly folk at the old people's home.

Cecil was in a self-contained unit within the 'village', so was more able-bodied than most. His sons lived overseas with their own families, so Cecil didn't have many visitors. He loved fishing and growing tomatoes, but he was a crotchety old man. I visited him three times before I gave up. Well, I was actually only in his presence the first time. The second time I visited he didn't want to see me, and the third time he told the nurses to tell me he was asleep, so all my findings are really just based on one visit.

I knocked on the door of his unit and Cecil opened it. He stared at me and, after I introduced myself, he told me I might as well come in. He complained about all the staff at the facility. He then spent some time looking at his neighbour through the blinds in the living room.

His mood improved, however, when I chose to comment on what looked like a plastic tennis racket. But this was no plastic tennis racket, my friend. This was a gift he had received from his granddaughter the last time she had been in the country. It was, in fact, a fly-killing device.

He picked it up, deftly spinning the handle and grabbing it again, not unlike a Wimbledon champion. 'Ya see, how it works is it electrocutes them. It's fantastic.

'Where are the little buggers?' he whispered as he scanned the room.

Then he spotted one resting at the top of the curtains. He made short work of it, swinging the racket and connecting it with the fly. The racket crackled just a little, then Cecil watched the fly's carcass fall to the carpet where he left it.

'Isn't it fantastic?' he said.

He shuffled towards the mantle. 'Oh look, there's another bugger.'

As a 17-year-old, I couldn't see the fly. But, as I've said, this special breed of Kiwi has brilliant eyesight when it comes to our buzzing friends. This time the fly caught his movement and flew off. With three desperate swipes of the racket, Cecil managed to get it.

'Ya see,' he told me, 'flies are very attuned to movement, and sometimes they can tell you're going to move even before you decide to.'

I nodded, trying to work that one out.

'Sometimes I just wait like this,' he said, holding the racket mid-air. 'I just wait. And wait. Then one comes along, and I get it!' This was accompanied by a quick swing of the racket.

'My daughter-in-law,' he said, shuffling to his La-Z-Boy chair, 'got me one of those timer fly sprays.'

With much effort, he lowered himself into his chair, then – using the momentum of his falling body – he grabbed the lever on the side and yanked up the leg rest. He sat back comfortably, his legs up at right angles to his body. 'You seen them?' he asked.

'Seen what?'

'Those timer fly sprays. Keep up.'

'Oh, I'm not sure.' At this point I was silently panicking, desperate to say the right thing.

'There's a little knob,' he explained. 'I wonder if it's still around here somewhere. I could show you. Anyway, it's got this knob so you can program how often it sprays. And I put it for fifteen minutes. Though I actually question if it was done on a timer or whether it was done on a sensor. I think it was actually spraying when it sensed movement because I put it for every fifteen minutes. And I put it there, on top of the fridge, but whenever I went to get something out of the fridge, it would bloody well spray me in the eye. Every time! So, I think it might've had a sensor. If it was a sensor, it must've thought I was a bloody big fly.'

That set him off. He laughed away until he was wheezing, and I think his false teeth might've dislodged.

'Ooh,' he said, 'there's one.' Cecil pointed to the coffee table, but I couldn't see a fly.

He anxiously tried to get up off his seat, but eventually he sighed. 'Here, you take this,' he said, proffering me the electrified tennis racket.

I sat up and the fly floated away.

'Careful!' Cecil warned me.

I took the racket and scanned the room. Where had the fly got to?

'On impact, you've got to push the button on the side,' he informed me. 'That's how the shock happens. Ooh! There it is!'

I followed to where his gnarled finger was pointing and saw a fly flying in a circle in the middle of the room. My problem was I was too tentative and gently pawed at it with the racket.

'Do a swipe!' Cecil yelled. 'Do a bold swipe, son. Don't be afraid of it.'

I did a bolder swipe but forgot to push the button on the racket's handle. It connected with the fly and just brushed it away. It flew out of the room.

'You were meant to push the button on impact!' Cecil informed me.

From that point on, any semblance of camaraderie had dissipated. He had lost all faith in me. I was like a lily-livered soldier in the barracks, who had disappointed his colonel. In writing this, I think I now understand why he didn't want to see me again.

THE OFFENDED AND THE OFFENSIVE

There was a woman in my childhood small town of Matamata – that's all the clues I'm giving – who would cry at the drop of a hat. Let's call her Trish. She'd cry because the people around her had offended her in some way. Often, they wouldn't even realise they'd offended her.

In this scenario let's call the offending party Gary. Now, Gary has just made an offhand comment about Trish's ambrosia having more marshmallows than he was used to. He didn't say this with any particular attitude towards the ambrosia. In fact, in no way did Gary find the ambrosia unsavoury. It was just heavier on the marshmallows than usual.

When he made the marshmallow comment, Trish's lips tightened and tears sprang to her eyes, then she excused herself from the room. In her mind, Gary had just made a dig at her and her ambrosia-making skills.

A few minutes later, having composed herself, she returned to the room where she managed to get through the rest of dinner, all the while waiting for another dig from Gary.

If she was lucky, he would make yet another comment. Maybe something like, 'How's the new job going, Trish?'

Trish would answer politely, but in her mind, she was curating a narrative in which Gary's question implied that Trish was somehow deficient for not having stayed in her previous job.

With dinner over, Trish gets into the car with her husband and he knows something is wrong. He asks if she's okay, but she simply sits in stony silence, or says, 'I'm fine, Brent.'

Half an hour later, though, she'll let loose. 'Never have I been so offended. If Gary wants ambrosia done his way then he should bloody do the ambrosia next time.'

Her husband then spends the rest of the evening trying to placate Trish, assuring her that Gary hadn't meant anything by his comment. Bad move.

'Why are you never on my side?' Trish hisses. 'You're always on someone else's side.'

Brent bites his tongue and agrees that Gary had indeed made a slight about her ambrosia.

Trish then decides that she and her family will no longer attend any events that Gary is going to be at. This will result in Gary's wife, Valerie, phoning Brent to ask what's happened.

Brent relays the ambrosia situation.

Valerie then makes Gary ring up Trish to apologise.

Then at the next event Gary will say something else that offends Trish, and so the cycle continues.

I once worked with a fellow who would take offence at a societal level. This guy wasn't about individual slights, he was offended on behalf of minority groups. He was a straight, white, middle-class guy who loved crying as much as Trish did.

Once I was doing a silly walk and he told me that it was 'not necessarily racist, but it was "problematic"'. Somehow, he'd assumed I was trying to walk like an African American. Scared of offending anyone, I apologised profusely and never walked like that again (though I'm not quite sure how specifically African Americans walk).

Another time, he showed up to work crying because of how unfairly the LGBT community in Brazil were treated. Then there was the time he called a work mediation meeting because he'd overheard two male co-workers discussing the female anatomy and he'd found it offensive. On a theme day at work, the same two men came dressed as Mexicans in colourful ponchos and sombreros. Our hero took huge offence to that, spending the whole day saying how offensive it was and how upset he was by it.

On the flipside, there are people out there that love to be the ones doing the offending. I wish I had their confidence, but not necessarily their way of expressing that confidence.

I worked with another guy who would go up to people and say, 'Do you want to see my girlfriend?' Then he'd proceed to show them graphic hardcore pornography. He'd mock our Pacific Islander and Indian co-workers by imitating their accents. He'd casually slip into an 'Asian' accent for no particular reason. He'd belch at any given opportunity, and he'd regularly mime graphic sexual acts, both heterosexual and homosexual, in front of all manner of people. His audience would be so shocked that someone could behave like this, that they wouldn't know how to react, so they'd laugh along politely whilst looking both pained and offended.

Then there are those individuals who are both offensive *and* easily offended. They usually find themselves behind a desk at a radio station or on a television show. One would assume, from the musical stings leading into their shows, and from all the branding around them, that they are journalists presenting news. But they are far from that. They are opinion men, usually aged 45 to 60. Always white. And always with an inflated belief in what they offer to the world. These guys usually live cushy lives in the city, but fancy themselves as 'men of the people', small-town salt-of-the-earth straight-talkers. They sell themselves as 'saying what the rest of us are too afraid to say out loud', and these statements are usually racist, homophobic, misogynistic, ageist or hating on the poor.

I listened with rage as one such prominent fellow had an argument with a young politician about legalising marijuana. She was for it, he was against it. A back-and-forth argument took place, which he soon began to lose, so he kneecapped her with the statement, 'No one is going to listen to you until you've had some life experience. When you've had three kids then you can come back, and we can talk about this. Because, at the moment, you don't have a leg to stand on.' And that was the closing statement to their discussion.

These guys like to throw punches about dole-bludgers, the nanny state and mental illness not being real, and that 'the Maoris' should take responsibility and stop their whingeing about the Treaty.

They can throw punches all over the place, but they are quick to play the victim. 'How dare you say that I am misogynistic?!', 'By saying that I'm racist you're showing that you, in fact, are misogynistic,' and 'Reverse racism exists, and I am the biggest victim of it.'

What I've never understood is the fact these men have a huge audience hanging off their every word. The guys I'm talking about are blazer-over-T-shirt-wearing, leather-pointed-shoe-donning, central-city livers, who surely aren't representative of 'middle New Zealand' who wear Swanndris and gumboots. But I guess if you say 'I'm just saying what everyone else is afraid to say out loud' often enough, people will start believing you.

THE LOVER OF ALL THINGS MAORI

When I was at high school, the kapa haka group was very strong. Everyone loved it when they performed at assembly. All the girls would swoon when the boys did the haka, and there was always a titillating thrill when the boys moved through the girls towards the audience. But at the end of the row of girls I couldn't help but notice the skinny girl with reddish hair, pale skin and freckles. Let's call this treasure Siobhan.

She was scrawny but still belted out the waiata at the top of her voice. At the time, I assumed she had some distant Maori ancestor, but, no, she was simply a Lover of All Things Maori. I later found out she had no Maori ancestry because some other white girls bullied her about it with a noticeably racist undertone. This bullying simply made our heroine dive further into her te reo studies and kapa haka practices.

Siobhan's family were Irish Catholic. There were six kids and two very devout parents, but our heroine seemed to reject all of that in favour of staying with her Maori friends and their families. I never really got to talk to Siobhan or work out her psychology, but I do remember her further back in primary school. We were making poi out of plastic bags and different coloured wool plaited together for the tassels. Her face lit up as she twirled them for the first time. She constantly pored over Peter Gossage's books *How Maui Slowed the Sun* and *How Maui Found His Mother*. I, on the other hand, was far more interested in Joy Cowley's nightmare-inducing book *Hatupatu and the Birdwoman*.

Cut to adulthood and I've come across several more women who are Lovers of All Things Maori, or, in one case, all things Moriori. When I ventured over to the Chatham Islands – a trip I recommend for everyone – I was invited onto the marae, where a petite woman addressed us all in the Moriori language, then translated what she'd said into English. She was strawberry blonde and freckled and wore a T-shirt emblazoned with an ancient Moriori tree carving. She was really clued-up on the history of the Moriori and the stories that had been passed down about them and their peace-loving ways. She knew all about their lifestyle and how they had subsisted on these windswept islands. She detailed their reliance on seals for food and how their only carbohydrates came from a gruel made out of fermented karaka berries, which are poisonous.

I assumed she was of Moriori descent and that she had lived on the island her whole life ... but no, she was Pakeha and had grown up in suburbia somewhere on the mainland. When she met her husband, who identified as Moriori, she had plunged headfirst into learning everything she could about his culture. Their children were devoutly raised as Moriori and she was a huge advocate for the reclamation of the reputation of their people.

Yes, she was Pakeha, but she said she identified as Moriori now and that was all that mattered. Meanwhile, the British lecturer in genetics who was seated beside me, a quietly spoken man who burnt in the sun within seconds, kept muttering under his breath about what he considered her 'wishy-washy approach' to the topic to which he had dedicated his life.

Back on the mainland, I have some dear Pakeha friends who are Lovers of All Things Maori. One embraced te reo very early on and became hugely proficient at it. My Maori friends tell me they tense whenever she approaches because she always addresses them in te reo and they're not always as fluent as she is.

Another friend filled her apartment with Maori art, took her Maori boy and girl dolls in traditional garb everywhere she went, had a traditional Maori design tattooed on her lily-white skin and ditched all her shopping bags for woven flax kete. She has never been overt about it, but I think, deep down, she wanted a living breathing Maori doll of her own. She hunted out a Maori man and had three children with him pretty bloody quickly. She claimed to 'have known he was the one when she met him'. I don't know what he thought. To be honest, I think the most important prerequisite for her before they embarked on a relationship together was that he was Maori. Turns out he was lovely, though.

Before they got together and had their progeny, she was adamant that her future children would be in bilingual classes, and that's exactly what happened. I mean, I'm all for goal setting and achieving your dreams, but everyone else in this woman's equation seemed as if they were simply players in her passion for the Maori culture. I've since established that the husband/father is quite happy to have a forthright, driven wife telling him exactly what she wants from him.

SMOKERS

I have always been attracted to Smokers, both romantically and friendly-y. Not that I have ever smoked, yuck, no way. But I've always hung out with Smokers. They're the best.

There was a period of time at intermediate school when the bell would ring for interval or lunch and I would venture out to sit with the bad girls and the gay boy (chubby with dyed black hair, with his fringe covering his eyes so that he could hide from people). I was there because I had no other friends at the time, and I was desperate. They also used to make me laugh a lot, so there was a great silver lining. The ringleader (remember Joanna?) had her tongue pierced. She was 12, and she had a tongue piercing. She would constantly be playing with it in class, sliding it back and forth between her front teeth. She did this to such an extent that she developed a hole in her teeth at the intersection of the front four. This meant she could slide the tongue ring through that hole without any resistance from pesky pearly whites.

Anyway, I would sit with the Smokers, agreeing with anything they said. I did this so that I didn't draw attention to myself, get kicked out and have no friends again.

I distinctly remember Joanna pulling out a brick of cigarettes. They're illegal now, but back in the day when you passed through customs, you could buy a brick of cigarette packets: 12 packets of cigarettes held together in a bigger packet. Anyway, Joanna's mum had just been to 'Oz' and had bought the brick duty-free on the way home for her 12-year-old daughter. I guess the reason she did that is to save on the tax Joanna would otherwise have paid.

Later in life, I found myself gravitating to Smokers again. I get it, it's an instant icebreaker – head to the smokers' area, ask to borrow someone's lighter and you're away. I also appreciate how smoking is the only time straight white men can express themselves. Driving around town, I see them smoking outside their place of business, or outside the hospital, or outside a bar, and they are completely uncensored. They'll take a drag on that cigarette with a pained expression, look up into the sky and shake their head, questioning their life choices or despairing about how things have played out, their eyes glassy and their minds ticking over. You don't usually see straight white men expressing themselves like that but give them a cigarette and you'll see it all.

Female Smokers seem to love to chat. The handful I know love to fold their arms beneath their bosom and take a deep drag. They'll hold that inhalation deep in their lungs, nod and dab a finger at you, indicating that they have something great to add to the conversation, then they'll lean far away from you (through politeness) and exhale and lean back in so they can carry on with their natter.

In my experience, smoking also seems to help with problem-solving. I've been in many a creative group where, whilst trying to nut out a problem, we'll feel like we're at an impasse, then the Smoker/s in the group will excuse themselves for a quick cigarette break whilst the boring non-smokers stare at the wall feeling useless. Invariably, the

Smokers will come back into the room with 'I've got it! I've got it.' They'll have come up with a solution – all thanks to stepping out for a smoke.

Then there are the lifelong Smokers. Tobacco and tar oozes from their very being. Long-term smoking seems to mould women's bodies in a specific way. Every lifelong female Smoker I've met has a thickening around the waist and very skinny legs. Their leopard-print tights just seem to hang off them, therefore not really being 'tights'.

I knew an old guy, let's call him Al. He didn't have male pattern baldness – his scalp was just completely hairless. It clearly wasn't through alopecia because he had eyebrows. He seemed to be about 85, but it's possible he could've been 70. He always wore a cheese-cutter cap and button-down, short-sleeved, patterned shirts. He smoked inside his apartment and had a boxer dog running around all over the furniture. As a result, the whole place smelt like utter hell. You'd have to take a huge gulp of air before stepping inside.

After you'd visited him, you'd basically have to take off your clothes before getting in the car because they were so drenched in the pong. You'd drive home naked, via a public rubbish bin, into which you'd throw your clothing, so it had no chance of contaminating your wardrobe at home.

Al was the first person I noticed who lit his next cigarette with the dying embers of the previous one. I found that very efficient. He ended up getting tongue cancer and having part of his voice box removed, so he had the hole in his throat.

He had to have a machine to help him speak, but he kept smoking, exhaling through his throat hole. Then part of his jaw had to be removed. But he kept living. He made it into his early nineties, having gone through several generations of boxer dogs. Eventually, he died of emphysema, but he was smoking until the end.

Many years after his death, I read an article about how each cigarette takes 11 minutes off your life. It made me think about how old Al would have actually got if he hadn't smoked – 123 is my calculation.

As the laws on tobacco get tighter and we get closer to it being banned altogether, I mourn the loss of the Kiwi Smoker. Smoking just lends itself to such specific characteristics. I wonder if it will be replaced with another vice. I bloody hope so.

THE SHY GIRL

I met a Shy Girl on the first day of my first year at university. She was in the same hall of residence as me. Let's call her Catherine. She had big front teeth, which she struggled to cover with her top lip. She was clearly out of her comfort zone. Whenever anyone looked at her, she'd blush and swallow painfully. I introduced myself and she whispered her name. I didn't hear it the first time I asked. Nor the second time. And I decided to not ask a third time.

'What are you studying?'

'Music,' she said, with an upward inflection like she was asking me a question.

'Oh great. Is that for singing? Or …?'

'Xylophone,' she said. She was warming up to me a little. 'My secondary instruments are the recorder and the triangle.'

I almost choked on my very sugary alcopop, which is what we were all drinking during our first meet-and-greet.

'What did you say your secondary instruments were?'

'The recorder and the triangle.'

'Can you actually study those?'

She nodded and blushed.

'Awesome,' I said, downing some more of my alcopop.

Catherine was always up for socialising. She was far too shy to initiate anything, but whenever anyone asked her to join in, she'd come along and say nothing. She would laugh, though. She had a great sense of humour. And when she laughed she'd always cover her mouth with her hand, like she was hiding her big chompers.

I grew very protective of Catherine. How could one not? She was a timid little bird out in the big wide world. She had come from a tiny town in the Wairarapa where she knew everyone. And now she knew nobody.

After the first semester, our floor at the hall of residence had a big party. Each group of five bedrooms was called a pod and during the party each pod had to entertain the rest of the floor for half an hour. To make it extra special, each pod had a theme for their alcohol and their decorations.

Catherine's pod had the best theme. It was 'mad scientist'. They all frizzed their hair and were wearing lab coats. They served blue alcopop in test tubes. Isn't that genius? Anyway, Catherine got absolutely wasted. She was downing those test tubes like nobody's business. It was then that we saw a whole new side of her. She was crass. She was loud. She was dancing crazily and then dancing sexily. She was attempting to pash guys … then she comatosed in the bathroom. When she woke up, she was all tears as she vomited. She got put to bed as everyone else moved on to the next pod.

The next morning, Catherine came down to the food hall wearing sunglasses. She gave a timid smile and ate her breakfast, pausing after every few mouthfuls to breathe through the nausea.

We didn't see 'wild' Catherine again until the end of the year when there was a repeat of the mad scientist night. The rest of the time she could be heard gently practising the xylophone or recorder or triangle in her bedroom and seen blushing at the slightest interaction with someone.

Adult Shy Girls aren't around very much. I mean, they must be somewhere quietly going about their lives, but you'll never see them because they're so timid.

You usually only see them earlier in life at institutions they have to attend, like school. And, boy, did we have some Shy Girls at my high school. There were two who fascinated me. They were part of a larger group of girls that we'll call the Misfits.

The Misfits were a hodgepodge collection of all the miscellaneous weird girls. The morbidly obese girl, the tiny one who still had her milk teeth, the girl with a heart problem that meant she was kinda webbed from her jaw to the edge of her shoulders. Those kind of people. I *loved* them, but boy did they get a hard time from everyone else. Thankfully, they had each other, I guess.

Within the group there was, let's call her, Rochelle. She was very tall but had a stooped neck. She also had frizzy ginger hair, freckles and the biggest buck teeth I had ever seen. Her sister, let's call her Shelley, was also part of the Misfits. She had a thin torso, huge hips and thick, thick hair she would wear like John Travolta in *Grease* for some reason.

My two favourites in the group? Let's call them Josephine and Denise. There was a rumour swirling around that Josephine was terrified of birds, so everyone would squawk at her. She never said anything in retaliation … or anything at all, really. Like, she was the quietest person possible, but she did partake in our primary-school choir.

The choir sang in the town centre at Christmas time and timid little Josephine was there desperately looking through the crowd. It was only after we'd packed up and were about to head back to school that she saw her misfit family amble down the road towards us. (Imagine a wheelchair-bound grandfather, morbidly obese brother, a father with a peg leg … that sort of family.) They'd missed her performance. It broke my heart. Instead of running over to them and letting them explain the situation, Josephine simply followed the rest of the class back to school.

Josephine's best friend Denise was my absolute favourite. She had permanently greasy hair, which was parted down the middle, and thick milk-bottle glasses that always had a greasy sheen to them. At school, the most popular way for the girls to wear their dresses was as short as possible. But Denise must've inherited a hand-me-down from someone six times larger than she was. Long skirts are fine for a uniform, but this one's waist came to her lower thigh and the bottom flapped around her legs awkwardly whenever she walked. It was an absolute triumph.

Many years later, I saw Josephine and Denise working at my hometown supermarket. I waved at Josephine, but she pretended not to notice me. She hurried back into the bakery, with a hairnet over her mousy hair. But I found Denise stacking some shelves and said hello. She proved to be very chatty. I'd always thought that she was on the dim side, but she held a very normal conversation with me, except for the fact that she told me she was learning naturopathy through correspondence … otherwise she was quite 'normal' and she even had her hair grease under control.

CHRISTIANS

In my experience there are two dominant types of Christians. There are the old-school Christians, who are in various states of decay, shuffling – occasionally using a Zimmer frame – to their local church on a Sunday. Their heads are permanently stooped, either from constantly bowing at church on Sunday, or from early onset osteoporosis. Their minister, invariably younger than they are, writes impassioned sermons, which the unanimated congregation doesn't react to, then greets them all kindly as they venture out at the end of the service.

At the other end of the spectrum are the new-school Christians. They come in various sub-categories. My favourite of these was a Kiwi girl who my brother hung out with in London. A devout Christian, she invited him to a Sunday service, promising him it 'wasn't like your usual service'. It took place in the same theatre where the Queen musical, *We Will Rock You*, played.

According to my brother, the service was punctuated with various pyrotechnic displays. This church's God was funky, he was fresh, he was rocking. Also, according to my brother, this church's God was very money focused. The preacher apparently spouted off about how much God loved money, and how much he loved his followers accruing it. Apparently, the Christian friend muttered 'Amen!' after every statement and wrote down every money-loving pearl of wisdom in her notebook.

At my school, there was a Christian Group. Lovely people. Funny people. Smart people. People who just couldn't quite infiltrate any other strata of the social ladder because of their love of the Beloved. They had all the right clothes and were good at sports, but that currency just didn't compute with the rest of the school. Everyone else had a slight wariness towards them, especially when these Christians would tense whenever anyone said, 'Oh my god.'

For some reason I got involved with these Christians and was invited along to their morning interval prayer meeting. I tried to approach it with an open mind. Unfortunately, they all turned on me when I asked, 'Why doesn't God just make his presence known and then we can all get on with it?'

For this, I was chastised with various phrases like, 'That's what having "faith" is all about.'

My favourite Christian at the time ran the youth group attached to the Anglican Church my family only attended for Midnight Mass at Christmas. I can't remember his name, but I do remember him being slight of frame. He had a ready smile and a distinct pallor. He travelled from Hamilton every week to get the local Matamata teens excited about God.

He called me once to invite me along to a pizza-making night in the Church's rumpus room. Being a 13-year-old people-pleaser, I found it hard to say no. Next minute, I was standing outside the rumpus room. That night, I'd made the mistake of taking fashion advice from my sister. There's no way around it, I looked like a cowboy – without the hat, thankfully.

I made my way inside and recognised some other students from school. They were slightly older and cooler than me. They weren't members of the Christian Group – somehow downplaying their faith, they'd managed to become part of the much cooler Cool Group. One of the girls asked me why I was dressed like a cowboy and the cool boys sniggered. I spent the rest of the night walking around as a mound of hot shame.

The Christian youth leader, let's call him Neil, had an air of desperation about him. He would laugh at jokes, as I find a lot of Christians do, even though he didn't find them funny. Why do they always seem to smile politely through various things they actually find blasphemous?

We made the pizzas – with spaghetti and pineapple on top – then we sat around talking, all while I was feeling very self-conscious about my cowboy outfit. Neil craftily managed to bring the conversation around to God. His crafty segue was talking about us sharing the pizzas and how Jesus shared bread with everyone. I mean, it was a nice message. I looked around the room at the six other teenagers who had chosen to attend, and I didn't want to share my pizza with them.

At the end of the night, my sister picked me up. Despairing at her choice of clothes for me, I vowed never to go back because the boys had sniggered at me. That didn't stop Neil calling me up every single week for months, asking me to come along to the next event.

Two months later I relented. He'd organised a van to take some young Christians to Rotorua to do the luge, which is kind of like a downhill go-kart. As we piled into the van, I was told the 'cool kids' no longer attended. Instead, there was a fresh group of eight teenagers. As we drove to Rotorua, I was quietly informed by the others that they weren't Christians, they were simply using the opportunity to go to the luge for free.

As soon as we arrived at the luge carpark, the others got their tickets and ran off. Not wanting to be alone with Neil, I joined them. It was a fun time, racing down the mountain in our go-karts. Neil desperately tried to join in, and laughed along good-naturedly, though I know he didn't find being deliberately rammed by the others all that funny.

On the drive home, he pulled the van over beside the lake. He turned around in his seat and told us spending time with friends — just like Jesus did with his disciples — was important. Before he could continue, one of the other kids opened the van door and we all piled out. We ran like the wind into the lakeside reeds. Neil gave chase, laughing desperately.

The luge had been fun, but this was the ultimate. We spent an hour playing hide-and-seek where the seeker (Neil) really did not want to play. Eventually everyone grew tired of it and we got back in the van.

With 15 minutes before we were due to arrive at the Church carpark where our parents were waiting to pick us up, Neil tried his sermonising again. The three girls in the back completely ignored him and kept talking, the two boys in front of them were listening to a Discman. The other three in the front row, which included me, half listened.

That was the last time I attended youth group, but it didn't stop Neil calling me every week to see if I would come along. Eventually he asked me if I was still interested in youth group. Bravely, considering I'm such a people-pleaser, I said I wasn't, and he never called me again.

I've got a final Christian tale to share. Again, it's my brother's. He went to his final-year school social with a Christian girl, then attended the Christian Group's after party. Being the rebels they were, the Christian Group decided to play a drinking game ... but with water instead of alcohol.

My brother warmly recalls that even though it was non-alcoholic, the water still seemed to make the partygoers drunk. Perhaps the water had turned to wine? It really livened up the party as these hormonal, desperately horny, keen-to-sin adolescents really wanted to tip over into drunken, sexual debauchery, but somehow they managed to get through the evening with their purity intact.

THE HEAD GIRL

There appears to be a breed of Kiwi girls in their late teens who have a drive for excellence not seen in any other subset of New Zealand culture. They are hellbent not only on academic success but in success across the board, whether it be in sports or cultural activities. They want to be the best at everything, sometimes to their own detriment.

They want to be Head Girl of their school and will be bitterly disappointed if they don't achieve that status. They're on every goddamn committee and involved in every extracurricular activity they can get their hands on – the school ball organisers, the future problem-solving team, the debating club, the 'teens cleaning up the streets' committee, the 'let's visit the elderly at the old folks' home' committee. And they take it all *very* seriously. They will study too hard and discover the benefits of coffee for the first time. They will do very well in their exams but will beat themselves up if they get anything beneath an 'A'.

To clarify, there are the academic girls at school, the ones that always get A+s. They are a different breed to the Head Girl species. The A+ girls don't overly obsess with how they look and can't be bothered being on committees. There are also the sporty girls at school. They are a different breed. The sporty girls don't get involved in anything 'cultural'. There are the cultural girls at school. They are a different breed. The cultural girls don't give a damn about sports.

The particular breed I'm talking about is the all-rounder striving for absolute perfection. They strive for success in everything. Usually, none of this pressure comes from their parents, who will love them regardless. This pressure either comes from trying to keep up with their peers or from a burning hunger from within.

Speaking of hunger, these girls have a tendency towards eating disorders. Perhaps this is a physical manifestation of trying to be perfect, or perhaps they feel it's the only thing they really can control even though they want to be able to control everything.

There was one girl at my school, let's call her Summer, who wanted to be Head Girl so goddamn bad. She wanted to be Head Girl from the moment she started high school at the age of 13.

Whenever the subsequent Head Girls would address the school during assembly, I would watch Summer's eyes almost glaze over and her mouth gently move with their orated words, her face fixed in slight ecstasy. It seems every decision she made, from her first day at school, was to position herself to take that coveted role. She trained so hard to be in the A netball team even though she didn't like the sport. Netball, though, was a foundation of the school and every other Head Girl before her played it. She partook in debating because it was a good opportunity to hone the oratory skills that would be so necessary when addressing the school at every possible event.

When Summer was 14, she went away for the three-week holiday in the middle of the year and returned many kilograms lighter, because, let's face it, you're more likely to be voted Head Girl if you're attractive.

Eventually, she reached her final year and everyone who wanted to be Head Girl (or head boy) nominated themselves, then did a speech expressing why they would be appropriate for the role. Summer's speech was, of course, perfect. She had an amazing resumé, which no one could fault, but, in the end, it's a popularity contest, right?

Summer lost to the most popular girl at school, who was definitely the more chill option. That girl, let's call her Tracey, promptly had a party to celebrate at which she got completely wasted.

Summer did get to be 'cultural captain' of the prefects – but it just wasn't good enough. Sitting up on stage at assembly, she couldn't mask her glowering, cold hatred as Tracey gave her Head Girl speech.

Interestingly, Tracey went on to become a bodybuilder with a penchant for extreme tans.

Many years later, I met another one of these girls fresh from another high school. She was a beautiful woman of Samoan descent, who had aced all her exams and was studying to be a doctor. She had also been in some high-up netball team and had won some speech competitions. She was an over-achieving all-rounder. She was kinda annoying. I mean, she was absolutely *lovely*. She did everything perfectly. She was even the perfect friend. But there was this … unrealness. She was too polished. There was some sort of rigidity I wanted to tear down. I wanted her to be 'real'.

She easily glided into the second year of medical school, but then she had a breakdown. I'm not sure what triggered it, but her body threw in the towel. Her weight doubled, she failed her exams, then seemed to become a nymphomaniac and an alcoholic.

The med school was very worried about her and gave her a year off whilst she plunged into the dark recesses of existential crisis. I saw her six months into this spiral. She was clearly anxious to have run into me during a late-night plunder of the supermarket for indulgent treats. She wore a hoody and her greasy hair hung long in an attempt to hide her acne. I wanted to address this sudden change but decided she clearly didn't want to talk so we parted after a few pleasantries.

I met her two years later and she was back on top. She was doing well at med school and was looking great. And, miraculously, the rigidity I had wanted to smash had completely dissipated. She was chill, laissez-faire, but still killing it with her grades and exercise regime. So, essentially, she had even managed to do a nervous breakdown perfectly.

JUVENILE DELINQUENTS

Criminality? Sure, let's go there. Thankfully, I've never had a run-in with a criminal that I know of. I mean, there was that time a burglar broke into my apartment and stole a speaker, my passport and a bag of carrots. I didn't even realise for three days. I was living by myself at the time and didn't think it was strange that a pot plant had been moved from a windowsill. It was only when I went to have a carrot, I thought, 'Hang on a second!'

This begs the question – why did they need all those carrots? I can only assume the burglar needed their night-time vision to be at its best.

Anyway, let's talk about a specific subset of the criminal: the Juvenile Delinquent.

The first time I heard this term was when my grandmother shared a story of a boy 'with his pants around his knees' who had come up to her in the street.

He'd yelled 'Hello!' in her face and run off, tripping over his pants then hobbling away. She described him as a Juvenile Delinquent.

I then saw one in the flesh at the local DEKA (a department store back in the day). He was hovering around the stationery shelves with his hood down low over his face and the back of his hand running below his snotty nose. He couldn't have looked more suspicious if he'd tried.

Anyway, he took three calculators and hid them, not in the pouch of his hoody, but beneath the shoulders of his hoody, which made him look like he had severe shoulder pads. I watched as he casually tried to walk out of the store, raising his eyebrows at the security guard as nonchalantly as possible.

The security guard made one simple movement, grabbing him by the shoulder. The Juvenile Delinquent tried to make a run for it but could only manage one step before being dragged into the shop.

I continued on my way around town. On behalf of my class, I'd been tasked with buying an engagement present for our teacher. I ended up buying a white china vase detailed with two doves, ribbons and plastic pearls. Sorry for the tangent, but the afternoon we gave her the vase, she gave me a detention for talking during class. Furious that I'd gone out of my way to organise her engagement gift, I waited until everyone was out of the classroom and threw the vase into the rubbish bin. Talk about juvenile delinquency!

Anyway, before I managed to find that wonderful, wonderful vase, I saw the Juvenile Delinquent from DEKA loitering around the dairy. Terrified, yet curious, I went and asked him what had happened at DEKA.

He rubbed the back of his hand under his nose and proceeded to tell me he was banned from DEKA and that everyone there was a 'c**t'.

I asked him why he wanted the calculators. He thought he could sell them. I mean, he was quite forthcoming and polite to me before asking me if I had any money. I had $2 from each of my classmates (given to me to buy said vase) burning a hole in my pocket but I lied and said I didn't. I then walked off as delicately as possible with the coins all clinking against each other.

The Juvenile Delinquent went on to become a tagger and was caught by the police doing some graffiti at the back of the train station. I saw him again after he'd done his community service. He had no idea who I was, but he was very open about his crimes and what community service he had done – painting over graffiti, ironically. He'd also had a haircut and was wearing his pants to his waist this time. Not that that means anything.

Years later, I wrote my first play. It was inspired by two real-life Juvenile Delinquents from the small township of Huntly. My actor friend showed me the article about them, and I was intrigued, so I, a privileged white kid, wrote a terrible play (that my soul will forever cringe over) about two Maori kids who poured glue over local cats in Huntly then set them on fire. I then cast two privileged white kids to play these roles in the first production.

I did spend a lot of time researching young boys from the wrong side of the tracks to make the play authentic. As part of my research, I weaselled my way into a classroom at an institution where boys who had committed crimes went. The first thing that struck me was how sweet they all were. Yes, they were easily distracted and provoked each other endlessly, and the poor teacher had to have the patience of a saint, but they seemed to be genuinely lovely boys.

They had spent the past few months making up their own boardgames. I was invited to play with one. This particular boardgame-maker had blonde hair that erupted out of his head and a permanent scowl on his face. He talked us through the game, in which you had to roll a dice and move your counter forward. If you landed on a square that read 'you scored dak, move forward three squares', you would follow that instruction. But then you'd land on a square reading 'the pigs have chased you, go back five squares'. I didn't end up winning his 'Game of Life'. He did. But fair enough.

I left the class that day feeling like these boys were victims of circumstance or that the education system simply didn't cater to them. After they had gone, I beat around the bush with the teacher, trying to work out what their crimes had been. Turns out it was a lot of robberies and beating the shit out of people.

DOGS

Growing up in rural New Zealand, there was a brutal reality that if an animal didn't pull its weight it would be ruthlessly put down. If there was any inkling of weakness in a dog, it would be lethally injected, or, if you were more on the heartless spectrum, it would be taken around the back of the shed to have a bullet put through its head.

And then I met this diabetic dog. He was some sort of Alsatian mix and he didn't have the nicest of personalities. He was forever barking and seemed perpetually pissed off. But somehow, he had weaselled his way into the affections of his owners, a couple who were family friends.

Their lives suddenly became dictated by the insulin schedule. They would take turns racing home at lunchtime to inject the dog. This went on for years, but if you had seen this dog's gnarled face and angry demeanour, you couldn't help but think he wished it wouldn't. He hated being injected.

The first time I saw it happening to him, he must've already been diabetic for two years, with insulin coming on the regular. I watched the needle go in and he became ferocious. He savagely tried to bite his mother with his snarling teeth. She managed to snap her hand away just in time.

As she returned the cap to the syringe, she had quite a detailed conversation with him about how she was just trying to help him. He simply stared at her, his twitching lips sometimes rising to reveal some teeth. She behaved as if he were understanding every word, though.

Eventually he did end up dying, but not before maiming a neighbourhood cat and attacking an elderly woman who was passing by their house. He was buried in the garden – and everyone (except the old lady he attacked) was upset about it.

Unfortunately, I didn't attend his funeral, but I was at their house shortly after the sad passing and there was not one, not two, but three framed photos of him on the mantelpiece. The wife's eyes teared up discussing him. I realised at that moment that maybe I had judged this dog without really knowing him, but part of me wondered if the couple were projecting a whole lot of feelings onto an, if not perpetually pissed off, then at least neutral canvas.

I met another dog like him once. This one was called Whitey and he was a mean bastard. I think he was some sort of Scottish terrier, and he had half-crusted gunk permanently oozing out of his eye. He had two very elderly sisters looking after him. They would all visit in their extremely air-conditioned car.

The first time they visited, Whitey clambered out and headed straight over to our farm dogs and attacked them, even though he was half their size. He latched on to one of them with his teeth and just stayed there, causing the victim to cry out in agony. When that happened, a memory came flashing into my brain. I distinctly remembered being at Cubs (the young Boy Scouts) where we were taught that to make a biting dog release its jaw, you needed to insert a finger into its anus.

Whitey did not seem to be letting up on our sweet dog so, in front of some terrified onlookers, I tried to insert my finger into Whitey's anus. I finally managed to do it but didn't get the release I was hoping for, so my father stepped in and literally punched Whitey in the face. This managed to do the trick.

The second time Whitey visited he wasn't allowed out of the car, so he sat in the front seat just watching everything. Every time I walked past the car, he would stare expressionlessly then let out a tirade of aggressive barks, almost giving me a heart attack. Maybe this was payback for the anus incident.

When Whitey died – after going missing on a farm, only to be found two weeks later, stuck in a rabbit hole, stiff with rigor mortis – my family mercilessly joked about him. The elderly sisters, though, were very upset. One of them teared up when they told us about his passing. It made me think that Whitey maybe had a softer side that only a few were privy to.

One last dog, again a complete bastard – lovely dogs just aren't as hilarious, are they? Let's call this one Cherry. Belonging to a friend of mine, who we'll call Kirsty, Cherry had some chihuahua in her ancestry.

My soul would groan whenever Kirsty arrived with Cherry. That dog hated me on sight. Whenever I was around, she would whine and scream then try to hide within her mother's arms.

'I don't know what's wrong with her. She usually loves people,' Kirsty would say.

I'd smile and shrug.

It soon became noticeable to everyone else. I'd arrive at a party and Cherry would be there and would instantly start howling.

'Jeez, what have you done to Cherry?'

'Nothing.'

'She hates you.'

'I can see that.'

'Perhaps she was abused as a puppy by someone who looked like you.'

'Perhaps.'

Then it became a case of me being at a social event and I'd ask where Kirsty was.

'She was going to come tonight but she didn't want to leave Cherry alone, and she couldn't bring Cherry along because ...' And they'd shrug and everyone else would look at me with slight disappointment because they all love Cherry. I think some of them would have preferred her there over me.

Cherry lived to 17, which didn't help. She eventually developed huge cataracts on her eyes so she couldn't see properly. I thought this might improve our relationship but obviously I must've smelt like this man that abused her as a puppy. When she passed away everyone was sad. I thought it was maybe an opportunity to mend my relationship with Kirsty, but that has yet to happen.

COUNTRY LIVING

New Zealand has long been a primary producer. From Te Puke's kiwifruit to the Marlborough region's wine, from all that milk powder being sent to China to all that mutton being produced because apparently people are still eating sheep. In any case, we make a lot of food. To keep that engine turning, we need human labour, and people aren't just personality-less robots. Behind every carrot being machine-plucked from the ground is a tractor driver with his own hopes and dreams. Behind every home-spun alpaca sweater is a lifestyle-block owner who is living their best life. So let's meet the New Zealanders living and working in the country.

FARMHANDS

Farming is the backbone of New Zealand, right? And behind every great farmer is a very competent or very incompetent Farmhand.

The closest I've come to being a Farmhand was at shearing time on the farm. There I witnessed the Maori shearing teams elegantly manhandling sheep into every angle as they expertly removed their fleeces. The previously agitated sheep suddenly became calm under their steady hands, then left the shed with an expression that could almost be read as appreciation. I was 'sheepo' in one such situation. It was my job to get the sheep into the holding pen so the shearers could have easy access to them. I wasn't the best at it, and the shearers often had to wait for me as I hopelessly tried to get the sheep up to them. Even though they'd had to break their stride, they wouldn't fuss. They'd just look at me with glassy, deep eyes.

Finally, smoko would arrive. Smoko was break time and the shearers would all roll cigarettes and sit on the grass, eating bakery food my mother had bought. I would have a white icing-ed custard square then hope there would be one leftover so I could have it. But there never was. I'd always finish smoko a little earlier than the others so I could desperately pack the pens with more sheep before the shearers got started again.

I once house-sat a homestead on a farm because the owners needed someone to care for their dog whilst they were on holiday. Their dog had a neurological disorder that meant that when she got excited, she would suddenly stiffen and collapse. Her name was Wanda.

When I took Wanda for walks on the farm, being careful not to excite her, we would often pass the Farmhand working away. This guy, let's call him Aaron, had a nervous disposition, which was exacerbated by the fact he was in charge of this huge farm whilst his boss was on holiday.

The first time I walked down the farm, I found him on the tractor, cursing away. He'd jack-knifed the attached trailer, making it point at an impossible angle. He was constantly changing between first gear and reverse, moving the tractor mere centimetres each time. Aaron just couldn't get his head around the angles and was simply making the trailer even more jack-knifed. In the end, I helped him manually unhook the trailer and lug it into a better position. He was profusely appreciative.

Two walks later, I found he had driven the tractor into a bog and couldn't get it out. I made my way over and saw he had placed branches under the wheels in order to get some traction. It hadn't worked, so he seemed to have given up and was silently screaming whilst he floored the accelerator, flinging mud every which way. With a big push we managed to dislodge the tractor. He was profusely appreciative.

Another time, I found him standing on the race (the dirt track between the paddocks) with his hands on his head, his body completely still. As I got closer, I noticed the fence beside him was twisted and splayed. As I got closer still, I saw the tractor had rolled down the hill and was on its side.

'I didn't put the bloody handbrake on,' he said under his breath, tears brimming in his eyes.

We went and got the other tractor and some chains, so we could pull the original one back onto its tyres. The hill was so steep, though, that the topsoil came away beneath the tyres of the tractor we were on and we slid down and pretty much crashed into the first tractor. Meanwhile Wanda, the dog, got so excited she spasmed and collapsed.

We managed to get the chains into the right position and pull the tractor back onto its tyres. But then we had the nightmare of getting both tractors up the steep hill with the topsoil sliding away beneath us. I discovered weaving your way up very slowly was the best option. The Farmhand, meanwhile, tried to motor it up to the top in a straight line. He almost made it over the ledge at the top, but the tractor lost steam. At the last second, he slid all the way back to the bottom. He then tried the weaving technique and we finally made it out. Thank god.

As I got to the end of my stay at the farm, Aaron's partner – a plump, blonde woman who coached netball and was always smiling – came breezing over to the homestead. She invited me to dinner at their cottage. By this stage,

I'd basically eaten the homestead empty, so was happy for the invitation. I explained I was vegetarian and her face blanched. I told her not to worry. I just didn't eat meat. I ate everything else – but not meat.

'Fish?' she asked.

'No. No meat.'

'Chicken?'

'Chicken's not … no, I don't eat chicken.'

'Oh boy,' she muttered.

As I approached the cottage that night, I could hear her crashing some pans together and then yelling, 'Well, I don't know. What do people eat if they don't eat meat?'

I tentatively knocked on the door and Aaron greeted me. His hand was bandaged. He was vague about the details, but I gathered he'd had an accident with a calf pen.

His partner walked into the hallway with a strained smile. She explained that she'd found a recipe at the back of her recipe book for cheese risotto.

All three of us ate it and it was delicious, but it clearly left them unsatisfied. 'So, that's all you would have?' she asked me. 'Just like a … like a risotto …?'

'Yeah, or just vegetables, if need be.'

They were both baffled.

'I just feel like something's missing,' the Farmhand said, a bloom of red emanating into the bandage on his hand.

*

FRUIT PICKERS

Fruit Pickers, of course, come in a wide variety, but I want to address a particular subspecies of the fruit industry. They are the foreign backpackers who come for a season, make enough money to pay for their travel around the rest of New Zealand, then leave and never come back. Sure, they're not 'New Zealanders', but I feel backpackers lend an integral, rich thread to the Kiwi tapestry.

I once had the good fortune to pick apples for a season. During that time, I met the most incredible people. Yes, I was the only one who would get sunburnt, and yes, I seemed to be the only one who didn't have the required musculature to handle day after day of heavy labour. But, after various conversations, I found out that we all lay in bed at night picturing apples hanging from trees and contemplating how best to harvest them. Years later, I still have the occasional dream in which various things go wrong while I have to harvest a tree full of apples with the clock ticking. These things include the ladder malfunctioning, not being able to reach the very last apple, or all the apples rotting and turning into goop in my hand. Anyway, that's another story.

Through apple picking I became friends with a Canadian man and his Israeli girlfriend. Let's call them their actual names because I don't think they will ever read this. I never kept in touch with them, but I do hope they're still alive. Anyway, they were called Daniel and Adi.

They had perfectly tanned skin and white teeth, which I regularly watched severing into a crisp apple. Adi's hair was purposefully knotty, maybe borderline dreadlocked, with a few beads scattered amongst it. A week into knowing her, she shaved one side of her head, a fashionable decision of the time.

Daniel, on the other hand, was brunette with blonde streaks. (Side note: he told me he never washed his hair and that the oils just naturally sorted themselves out – and, damn, his hair was glossy. He told me it took a couple of weeks to reach the right equilibrium, so I attempted it. A month later, I looked like I had been swimming in canola oil. It spread from my scalp down over my body giving me an all-over permanent sheen. I just feel some people are naturally more oily, okay? And there's nothing wrong with that.)

When Daniel didn't have his hair up in a topknot, he would wear his hair tie around his wrist. Wrist adornments were a big thing for this couple – they had lots of bracelety things, ribbons tied around, things that looked like friendship bracelets and a few wristbands from various festivals they'd attended.

Adi always wore singlets and Daniel often went topless. And they were both so damned comfortable in their bodies.

What struck me most about Daniel and Adi was their approach to life and how different it was from my own and Susan's – she was another picker, who was saving for nursing school. When the four of us worked together to strip a tree, there I was worrying about the future, making plans for the coming year, working out how to pay rent, thinking through my various to-do lists. And there were Daniel and Adi without a care in the world.

I asked them if they had any must-sees during their time in New Zealand. They didn't. They then said that if I had any recommendations, they'd check them out. I went home and furiously googled 'Top things to do in New Zealand'. As a result, I suggested they visit Ninety Mile Beach in Northland. They went the following weekend. In fact, they went off to do something every weekend. They kept saying how beautiful our country was. I'd shrug. I mean, I'd heard Queenstown was beautiful, and the beaches can be nice.

They asked me if I knew anyone who could get them some marijuana. I went above and beyond trying to find them some, but my drug-dealing clout was minimal. The following day, I was very apologetic about it and they told me not to worry. In fact, their general demeanour was about not worrying – so much so, I felt guilty about worrying whenever I was around them.

They did their work without fuss or complaint and were so open to everyone who came into their lives. Whenever a new picker came, Adi and Daniel would give them the time of day without judgement. And the other pickers would do the same. It was just this beautifully non-judgemental, egalitarian society. It was beautiful.

And then it was over. The apples were all picked, and Daniel and Adi were heading to the South Island in a van they had managed to get running. I followed them on social media, and it was just beautiful vista after beautiful vista. I forgot about them for a while until they posted some photos of their travels in Namibia, where they were looking after some goats and fully appreciating life.

Many years later, I had a Mormon from Seattle couch surf at my place. He had the same gentle vibe. Just going with the flow, he was open to any adventure I suggested. He had an appreciation for the beauty that's around us all the time. His energy was so attractive, a calm quietude and assurance that things would work out.

We went for a walk through the park one day, and he pointed out a puriri tree I had walked past multiple times without ever taking any notice of. He said it was 'perfect'. Just then a kereru whomp, whomp, whomped in and started eating the berries, as if it had been waiting for my visitor to call 'Action!'. We stood there for a minute. After 30 seconds, I wanted to move on, but persevered and really took in the marvel before me. I guess it sometimes takes being aware of other people's outlooks on the world to realise what a beautiful country Aotearoa is.

CALF CLUB KIDS

Herding sheep through a gate is a delicate business. A dog is usually necessary, but they can also cause untold damage to the affair. You slowly edge the flock of sheep towards an open gate, on the other side of which is lush, fresh grass. The sheep should be able to see said grass if they just turn their herbivore heads to one side. They get closer and closer and closer to the open gate. Then they decide, for some inexplicable reason, to veer off at the last second. They run along inside the fence of the paddock you're trying to get them out of.

You yell at the dog to round them up. He tries his best but ends up splitting the flock into three: one large subset, one smaller subset and a lone lamb bolting off at great speed. The dog chases the lamb as it hurtles into the fence on the other side of the paddock. After much writhing and panic, and with the dog momentarily confused, thinking the lamb is prey and trying to kill it, the lamb manages to squeeze between the wires and runs into the wrong paddock.

Meanwhile, one of the sheep in the large subset has taken confident leadership and is taking her followers to the wrong gate. You focus on the smaller subset and run at them, bellowing weird noises as you attempt to herd them towards the correct gate. Just before they reach it, the sheep split into a further three subsets. Complete chaos ensues.

You get three sheep through the correct gate, then return to get the remainders. As you are doing so, the three successfully placed sheep wander back through the correct gate to rejoin their misplaced companions.

Cows are much easier to herd. Yes, they can panic. And yes, you want to assure them you mean no harm as they desperately run away from you even though you have no way of communicating that, but they tend to go in the right direction. But then there are the bulls. Bellowing deeply, or wheezing and kicking sand and soil backwards, they seem far more interested in intimidating each other, showing off their huge bulk, than letting you shoo them anywhere.

That's before we even get onto the offspring of these two species.

If you grew up in rural New Zealand, you might have just been lucky enough to attend the school calf club. This special day was a chance for farm kids to compete against each other with their pet calves. Lambs were also an option, as were kids. At our school, there was always a limited number of baby goats, which gave them an unfair advantage when it came to winning ribbons. But it was called *calf* club, so the other species can be damned.

As the wisteria bloomed and daisies moved softly in the breeze, farmers' utes were driven onto the school field. On the back of the utes were metal cages containing prize baby animals. At the head of the field were three pens created using electrical fence tape (not electrified in this situation), each held up in its four corners by fencing standards, which are metal poles with a loop at the top. These loops were covered in white or red plastic and were there to thread the electrical fence tape through.

The babies of the three species, and their child human trainers – the Calf Club Kids – competed against each other in a series of activities. First up was leading. This involved each Calf Club Kid walking their animal around the inner edges of the pen. The main pitfall of this was when the animal would dig its heels in and refuse to move.

Next up in the calves' section was the obstacle course. The Calf Club Kids would lead their calves around several tyres and through a gate. Then the lambs and kids would do what was known as 'Call, Follow, Run'. This involved an adjudicator holding the lamb whilst its child ran to the first corner then called for the animal to run to them. The main pitfall of this was when the excited animal would run in any direction except towards its trainer.

Finally, there was the grooming section. This involved the adjudicators, who all wore white lab coats if I remember rightly, looking over the animal in detail. (A trick my mother taught me was to polish your lamb's hooves with black boot polish before the competition.)

After each round, the adjudicators would award coloured ribbons for first (red), second (blue), third (yellow), fourth (green), fifth (peach) and sixth (brown).

Once when I was competing, there were seven lambs competing for six ribbons, so we ended up having sixth-equal, so that no one was left out. The littlest lamb in the competition, which appeared to be newly born (owned by a girl with braces called Shelley), got that ribbon every time.

At the end of the day, a champion calf, champion lamb and champion kid were awarded champion ribbons (baby blue with white tassels on the end and twice as wide as the other ribbons). They were also awarded a silver cup for god's sake, and then were invited to compete in the local A&P show, where they would compete against the best of the best from other schools.

The adjudicators were just parents who'd put their hands up to do it. They had no credentials to speak of. For two years when I was competing, one of the adjudicators was a mother of a competitor. That competitor (her daughter) took out champion calf both years running. And NO ONE ELSE SEEMED TO HAVE A PROBLEM WITH THAT!

I never did particularly well as a Calf Club Kid, and I felt pained by that. My elder sister had gone down in history with her champion lamb, Pebbles. The photo of her with Pebbles and all the ribbons and cups they won is still on the mantelpiece in the family living room. I only got half a dozen greens (fourth) and one blue (second) throughout my competitive baby animal career. As I was given the blue second-place ribbon, the adjudicator told me I would have won if I had petted my lamb when it ran up to me in the Call, Follow, Run section. The reason I never won was because I hadn't petted my beautiful lamb, Apricot. I still wear that guilt and shame to this day.

THE NUMBER 8 WIRE KING

How can one talk about New Zealanders without talking about the number 8 wire mentality? This is the idea that we can fix anything with a piece of number 8 wire. Number 8 refers to a size of wire, I believe … ?

Your Massey Ferguson tractor's falling apart at the seams? Put a ring of number 8 wire around the engine to hold it all together. That'll keep it going for another 20-odd years. Your power's cut out? Simply thread a piece of number 8 wire around the neighbour's electric fence and hook it to your power board. Your dentures have split in two? Simply solder them onto a curved piece of number 8 wire.

My grandfather was The Number 8 Wire King. His name was Stuart, but we called him Gang Gang because my sister – the eldest grandchild – pronounced Grandpa as Gang Gang and the name stuck. His wife, our grandmother, was called Bingar, which is slightly more of a stretch. Bingar/Grandma? Hmmm … I guess I can see how it happened.

Bingar died early on in the piece and Gang Gang had 20-odd years left in him. During which time, he had several girlfriends who would come and live with him on the farm. The periods of time between the girlfriends, however, involved him letting himself go. His eyebrows would grow every which way, he would use bailing twine instead of a belt, and he'd live off home brew and pickled onions.

One of my most enduring images of Gang Gang is of him soldering things together. He always wore a protective eye shield, but it would be lifted up off his face, so his eyes were looking directly at the intense white glow.

One of his girlfriends was called Von. She lived in Adelaide and I remember the day Gang Gang flew over to meet up with her. He took my sister and me aside and said he was going to be coming back with a woman. He was true to his word.

Von was an Aussie larrikin, who regularly had us laughing. She had dyed black hair, which she used to set with curlers. She was good for Gang Gang because she set up two rules: one, no smoking, and two, no scratching. A lifetime of working out in the harsh New Zealand sun had given him various skin deformities, which he was forever scratching until they bled.

Gang Gang and Von would spend six months in New Zealand and six months in Australia, so they could keep collecting their pensions in their respective countries. But Von's first six months here created a few problems. First of all, the bed wasn't big enough for both of them, but instead of purchasing a new bed, Gang Gang came up with a genius solution. He took two single mattresses and sewed them together with bailing twine. He told the rest of the family this with pride. I couldn't help but think through the icky mechanics of why they needed such a big bed.

Von also had trouble with her hips, so she found it difficult to get up and down from the couch. Gang Gang took several planks of two-by-four and screwed them to the couch legs, so there were these retro, leather-armed couches with scrap-wood two-by-fours jutting out of the bottom.

These made the couches hilariously high and allowed Von to basically tip herself forward and be standing, rather than having to laboriously pull herself up.

I guess this kind of resourcefulness and ability to calmly deal with a situation resulted from New Zealand being so isolated from the rest of the world. We had no one to rely upon but ourselves, and we often didn't have the access to tools or materials that other countries did.

I remember going out fishing with Gang Gang in the Coromandel. I had a great fear of the ocean and the creatures that live in it, but I never let anyone know. We were out there, fishing away, when suddenly the motor fell off the back of the boat. The bolts tentatively holding it in place were very rusty and had finally given up the goat.

Without missing a beat, Gang Gang leapt over and managed to grab the motor before it disappeared into obscurity, then he simply held it in place for our voyage back to dry land ... that voyage back, though, only took place after another hour of fishing.

Thankfully, this number 8 wire mentality has been passed down to the younger generations. One of my friends was moving flats and, without a tow bar on his car, he somehow managed to use his jeans to connect the trailer in through the open boot and around the back seat. It was my role to sit in the back seat and report on any tearing of the jeans, especially around the crotch area. I was very nervous about the whole thing, but he seemed very confident.

I presumed he would move his car at a snail's pace, his hazard lights flashing as he waved any other traffic around him. But he didn't. He hit the road at speed and even got to 60 kilometres in a 50-k zone. I don't think I breathed throughout the entirety of the trip. But we made it and he seemed unfazed by how precarious the whole endeavour had been.

Once at his new place, we manoeuvred the very stained, very old mattress in through the second-storey bedroom window using a pulley system of bungee cords and a crowbar, which he didn't mind plunging into the already fraying floral fabric of the mattress. When he did finally procure a bed frame for that mattress, it was a mishmash of multiple bedframes and a wooden crate.

The number 8 wire mentality also strays into the arts sector sometimes. I've done far too many theatrical productions where my gun was made of cardboard, or my gnarled legs (I was acting in a play version of *Misery*) were simply stockings stuffed with pieces of foam, or a movie camera prop was just a rat trap someone had found outside the venue. All of this was done as a result of budgetary restrictions or an inability to get the props sent over from America or Australia, or wherever, in time, but somehow New Zealand audiences buy into the imagination of it all and come along for the ride. I guess the conclusion from all of this is not only do we make do, but we make do ingeniously.

THE NO-NONSENSE FARMER'S WIFE

I met this woman once, who, after her husband had a truck accident, took over the running of the farm whilst he got back on his feet. One morning she was milking the cows and one stood on her hand with all its weight at a strange angle, essentially smashing it and shattering the bones. Instead of screaming, becoming hysterical or driving her tractor to the hospital like most people would, she simply wrapped her hand up in tape, finished off the milking, headed home and got the kids ready for school, waited for them all to get onto the school bus, then drove herself, with smooshed hand, all the way to the hospital. There, the doctor was shocked she hadn't passed out with the pain.

She was eventually sent to Waikato Hospital where she had screws put in her hand. She was pissed off she couldn't make it back home in time for afternoon milking, and she had to get her brother-in-law to come and do it for her. But she was back in the shed the next day – with cast on full display.

She never used that smashing of the hand to garner any sympathy or allow herself to go easy on the schedule. No way. She was still milking every morning and doing everything very capably. All of this has made her, in my opinion, a type of New Zealander who is basically the backbone of the country. It's the No-Nonsense Farmer's Wife.

Now I say 'farmer's wife', but, of course, I realise these women might have nothing to do with a farm – they may work in construction, the transport industry, or the bulldozing business. Mostly practical fields, though; a no-nonsense hairdresser doesn't have quite the same vibe.

I also realise that a woman shouldn't be defined by her relationship to a man, but the majority of these women I've met have indeed been married to a farmer – and their husbands would be completely hopeless without them because the No-Nonsense Farmer's Wife is so damned practical.

Here are some givens about the No-Nonsense Farmer's Wife:

1. They have no problem with killing things. Don't get me wrong, they're not bloodthirsty, nor do they kill unnecessarily, but if the situation arose, say a dog had been hit on the road and it looked like it would die, she'd calmly get out her rifle and put a clean one into its head. Or if the chicken population was getting out of control, she'd swiftly chase the rooster down and wring its neck, all with a set, determined look on her face.

2. They have no anxiety about manning heavy machinery. Say the forklift driver is on the dunny and someone needs to get their Hilux out of the garage, which is being blocked by the forklift. Our heroine will swiftly and expertly get into the forklift driver's seat to do what is necessary.

3. They wear make-up only when necessary. This entails some mascara and some lippy, and that's it – and it only comes out for weddings and funerals.

4. Speaking of funerals, these women are the ones who pretty much run the show. Sure, their dad has just died, but they'll be there making sure it all runs swiftly. I'm using the words necessary and swiftly a lot. It feels right because these women do what is necessary and they do it swiftly. I should add capably to the words that describe them because, my god, they're capable.

5. They have sensible haircuts, always on the shorter side. They might wear one bracelet and their wedding ring, and maybe a thin gold necklace, or maybe some gold stud earrings. But it's all very subtle. There are absolutely no unnecessary flourishes.

6. They can't get their head around modern anxieties. Why is that couple having such problems? Why not just shut up and get on with it? Why do people have weight problems? Why not just stop eating so much? Speaking of weight, these women usually have muscle tone and are on the slighter side. They're the ones who make the dinner because women traditionally make the dinners – and it'll be corned beef and three veg, or devilled sausages, or roast lamb with all the trimmings.

7. They don't change their behaviour or demeanour in different situations. If her husband drags her to New York because he's always wanted to go there, then she'll carry on as if she were still on the farm. She'll have no qualms about walking up to an obvious drug dealer and asking him for directions, then striking up a conversation about how he lives his life.

8. They don't want presents. You'll always hear them say, 'You didn't have to get me anything,' or 'Don't bring any presents, I don't want anything.' In fact, they rarely want for anything. If you take the gamble and buy her a scented soap for her birthday, it'll go into the bathroom cupboard and never be used because only heavy-duty Sunlight soap gets the grime out from under her fingernails.

9. They suit having sons more than they do daughters. Sons are practical and straightforward, so our heroine can get her head around them. Girls are a bit more tricky, and heaven forbid if the daughter is on the emotional side. Mother and daughter might well have a very difficult relationship.

10. And finally, our heroine's attitude to her own death is very practical. She'll make sure the deep freeze in the garage is full of frozen dinners for her husband for the coming years. She'll tell everyone not to make a fuss and bother at her funeral, but everyone will turn up to the service and be sad but also laugh at how goddamn swift, capable and tough she was. Nothing could get her down.

I guess my overall feelings about these women is that, sure, there are some real tough blokes out there, but, my god, there are some even tougher sheilas.

NOSEY NEIGHBOURS

The road I grew up on had a lot of 'peering through blinds'. By that I mean neighbours spying on each other with all the discretion venetian blinds allowed. Too many of them would stand at the blinds, forcing their index and middle fingers between two slats at eye level and prising them apart just so, so that they could get a good view. Their eyes would narrow as they watched their neighbours going about their business, and they would mutter quietly under their breath about how the neighbours were conducting said business. 'What's he doing out there? He only bloody mowed his lawn on Saturday. You're not meant to mow your lawns so regularly. It's not good for the lawn health.'

Two hours later: 'What the hell is he up to now? He can't leave that bloody lawn alone for five bloody minutes. It's like he's worried he'd turn away for two minutes and then turn back and it would be full of thistles.'

I didn't have much to do with the people on my long, rambling, rural road until my eleventh year when I decided to walk the length of it (alone) and ask my neighbours to sponsor me to do the 40-Hour Famine – a school scheme that raised money to send to starving kids in Africa.

During this ramble, most of the neighbours greeted me at their door with an air of mild irritation. One of them greeted me in his boxer shorts, and I'd heard female moaning moments before I knocked. It took me years to realise what had been going on in that particular situation.

I explained the parameters to all my neighbours – they would sponsor me from five cents to $2 for every hour that I lived off barley sugars and Just Juice (instead of eating any other food) and I would come back, collect the money and it would be sent to starving people in Mozambique.

Not one of them appreciated that sort of commitment, nor the idea of me coming back, so they just gave me the cash there and then. Oftentimes it would just be a handful of coins dumped into my sweaty palms. I explained that I was meant to come back and collect the money after I'd done the famine as that was an incentive to get me through the 40 hours. But they said they trusted I would be fine and sent me on my merry way. I still needed them to fill out the booklet, though, and would make them stand there as I counted out the handful of coins and tried to do the maths on how much it was divided by 40, as that was what they were paying me for each hour. I also had to get them to sign the book, and only then would I trot off their property.

This happened house after house until I approached the Gubbs' house. I'm not going to change their name as I presume none of the Gubbses are still alive. The Gubbs' house was at the end of a driveway, past various camellia trees smelling sweetly and buzzing with bees.

As the white house loomed before me, I noticed a gap in the living room's venetian blinds. Almost as soon as I saw the gap prised open by two fingers, it suddenly disappeared.

I knocked on the big door with the friendly 'rat-a-tat-tat' I'd decided to use on all the previous doors. After a few seconds I heard a 'Come in'. It was an authoritative voice, regal almost.

I tentatively opened the door and peered into the gloom. I couldn't see anyone straight away, but I slid my gumboots off and left them at the door. I crept inside and down the hallway, my ears straining to hear anything. Then I saw Mrs Gubb seated in the dining room. Her presence gave me a fright, but she sat there, erect, appearing almost staged.

'What is it?' she asked.

'I've come to talk to you about the Forty-Hour Famine. Do you know that most people in Mozambique only have one meal a day? And that meal isn't even nutritious.'

'Are you asking for money?'

I nodded tentatively.

'Have you been going around the whole neighbourhood?'

I nodded tentatively.

'What's that book?'

She held out her hand. I moved forward and gave it to her. She took the reading glasses hanging from a cord around her neck and slid them up over her eyes and proceeded to go through the book, analysing every page and every payment.

'Is that all the Van Husens are giving you?' she muttered. 'That's very cheap of them.' And 'Oh, you managed to get money out of the Houghtons? Well, good for you.'

As she continued looking through the pages, I scanned the room and realised it had been designed with an almost panoramic view of the entire road. The venetian blinds had been pulled to half-mast but I still had a clear view of the nearest neighbours' homes.

'How was Renee Johnson at number one eighty-nine looking?' she asked.

'Excuse me?'

'Has she lost any of the weight?'

I shrugged.

'I presume she hasn't,' Mrs Gubb said as she turned the next page. 'Oh yes, you managed to squeeze some money out of that tight bastard Mr Faulk. He doesn't spend any money on his house or car or clothing, so he must be loaded. Did you get a good look in his house?'

'Not really.'

'He must be sitting on a pile. Did he look like he was sitting on a pile?'

'I don't know.'

She turned a page of the booklet. 'Oh, Mrs Pemberton. She's stopped dying her hair, I see. It's aged her terribly as far as I can tell. What did you think?'

'I don't know.'

She reached the last page of the booklet then stood up. She moved to the blinds, prised two apart with her index and middle finger and peered outside.

'So, you're a Sainsbury boy, are you?' she asked.

'Yes.'

'Your mother hasn't been running past lately. What's wrong? Is she sick?'

'Umm.' I had no idea how to answer, so I shrugged.

Mrs Gubb didn't press me. She simply turned to face me and looked me over.

'This Forty-Hour famine will be good for you,' she said. 'But I don't think I'll sponsor you.' With that she handed back the booklet.

I was in complete shock. No one had rejected me yet. I didn't know quite how to manage it. I took the booklet and stumbled out of the house and across the road, where the next neighbour offered me a handful of coins. He told me not to bother going to the Gubbses because Mrs Gubb was a tight old bitch and I wouldn't get anything out of her. If only I had gone there first!

I started running regularly after that, in an attempt to look less like someone who a 40-Hour Famine would be good for. Every time I ran past the Gubbses, I could see two fingers prising apart the venetian blinds and I knew she was formulating opinions about me. I hope she approved of my transformation.

VEGETABLE GARDENERS

We are a nation of people, I deduce, that is a lot more connected with the land than most citizens of the world. If you don't make your living from the land, you're probably not too many generations away from people who did. I would argue that growing our own vegetables is in our

DNA. But within that vegetable gardening subset of society, there are various subspecies.

First off is the Hopeless Gardener, like me. Spring arrives and I have such lofty expectations. I buy the plastic pots, the potting mix and the baby tomato plants. And I seem to do everything right. To start with, whenever someone comes around, I happily show them the potted tomatoes and it's a real conversation starter about how to get the best harvest. By the end of summer, I can harvest one fair-sized tomato, one warped tomato the size of my thumb and a green tomato that has started to go mouldy. Those are the fruits of my labour from six tomato plants over the period of six months.

On the flipside are the Overly Successful Gardeners, who have so much success that their neighbourhood is showered in tomatoes and marrows for the months of February and March. They're usually of an older persuasion, maybe grandfathers who like to provide.

'Before you leave, let me get you some tomatoes? You like tomatoes? I'll get you some tomatoes … here ya go, that's twenty tomatoes in there,' they say as they pass over a jam-packed, slightly warped, blue ice-cream container.

'Oh, I couldn't possibly take all twenty,' you say, 'I wouldn't know what to do with them.'

'Nonsense. They'll go to waste here. We've got at least fifty times that on the plants. I've also thrown in three courgettes.'

They're not courgettes, though. They're full-blown marrows. Because courgettes are so tricky, aren't they? They're the right size for a day, then suddenly they're the size of a baby dolphin. Occasionally some string beans will be thrown into the mix – but they've been on the vine for just a few too many days. You attempt to cook them for dinner and they're so stringy you don't need to floss that night. You'll only get through three of the tomatoes and the rest will spoil and have to be thrown out along with the plastic bag of baby spinach you bought from the supermarket, fully expecting to use it to its full potential, within 24 hours. Instead, the outer leaves have yellowed and it looks like the mushier leaves are starting to kinda fizz.

The Overly Successful Gardener usually revels in the wonder of chutneys and relishes, handing over a jar (typically a recycled Pam's strawberry jam jar) with the date the relish was bottled written on the top. For months, you'll have it at the back of the fridge beside the olive jar opened a year ago, some half-used black bean sauce and the cranberry sauce you never finished at Christmas. Eventually, you'll drag the chutney out and slather it over some cheese or a cracker and marvel at the loose cut onion and sultanas within it. Delicious! Then you'll return the jar to the back of the fridge for another few months until the rim goes crusty. You'll throw it out when it becomes kinda fizzy.

If you're living with an Overly Successful Gardener, you will have experienced your own kind of hell. For a time, my mother had an asparagus farm and during asparagus season, whilst everyone else salivated over the sweet and tender spears, my siblings and I would inwardly groan at yet another healthy serving of all the C-grade asparagus that wasn't fit for sale. This would include the very wide and flat ones, the crooked ones and the mature ones.

I also vaguely remember a bumper crop of leeks in my childhood. Suddenly we were having leeks with every goddamn meal. Bless her, my mother did attempt to add variety – we had boiled leek, fried leek, coddled leek, chicken and leek puff pie, leek pizza, leek and ricotta lasagne …

Finally, there are the vegetable gardeners who are both very good at it but who also have a real understanding of supply and demand. Let's call them the Competent Gardener. They take you down the back of the section where stunning sunflowers stretch towards the sun, where three kale plants erupt in a dark green fountain, providing all the kale anyone would ever need, with corn growing high and cucumbers growing long. The plants seem to thrive despite the Competent Gardener's lack of anxiety. This subset of vegetable gardeners has an innate sense that the plants will be fine – and they are fine, enriching their carer with delicious pumpkins and bumper potatoes.

Occasionally the Competent Gardener will dabble in heritage varieties. They'll hand you a huge yellow tomato or one that is purposely green even when ripe. They'll dig up some purple potatoes and tell you they're good for mashing.

They'll hand you some beans mottled red and green and explain you'll just need to steam them then add a wad of butter.

You'll feel so healthy and organic as you imagine eating these vegetables with eggs provided by the Japanese silky hens scratching around in the sun with their topknot hairdo flapping every which way. But then you realise, these hens were probably fed with fizzy old chutney from the fridge ...

BAD CONVERSATIONALISTS

I have spoken to a fair few foreigners in my time. They regularly share a specific observation about New Zealanders with me. Apparently, us Kiwis have a warm energy and are very friendly – but only to a certain level. If they try to get deeper with us or try to create a lasting friendship, they find it impossible. They find us closed off, standoffish even. I found this information quite hard to process. Are we really like that?

Coupled with that, I've had foreign friends from the feistier nations – the United States, Mexico, Brazil – complain to me that New Zealanders simply don't say what we're thinking. Here *they* are, blurting out exactly how they feel and what they want. Meanwhile their New Zealand counterparts clam up and avoid eye contact. We are closed books.

I guess, to a certain degree, I agree. In my own experience, there is a subset of New Zealanders who I refer to as Bad

Conversationalists. They are usually white, straight men of a rural persuasion, and they are definitely closed books.

I got a full dose of the Bad Conversationalist a couple of years ago. A friend invited me to the Coromandel for a long weekend. She had rented an Airbnb by the beach for her and a few friends. I was excited. She was great company and I liked a lot of her friends. I was most excited, however, by the three-hour car trip there. I was excited that I would be all on my lonesome. For three hours. I'm not a huge fan of travel. I mean, I love being at different places, but getting there is such a drag. But this car trip was a welcome delve into solitude. I could listen to Katy Perry on repeat and sing to my heart's content. I could listen to podcasts or I could just let my mind wander.

Then, on the morning I was to drive down, I got a text message from my friend, who was already in the Coromandel and asking if I could possibly pick up her brother from the airport and drive him down with me.

I felt my stomach drop. I had to control the loudest, most pissed-off sigh from leaving my lips. Driving a stranger down in my car, for three hours, just the two of us alone, was the last bloody thing I wanted to be doing. But, of course, I had to say yes.

I had to befriend her brother on social media, so we could coordinate pick-ups, etc. His online photos consisted of him holding fish or standing over dead stags with a thumbs-up. Being a vegetarian urbanite, I knew I was in for a rough ride.

I parked my lavender Honda Jazz in the airport carpark and waited for him at the arrivals gate. Eventually he emerged and I waved him down a little too enthusiastically and introduced myself. To which he replied, simply, 'Sweet.'

I asked him how he was.

'Not bad.'

I asked him how his flight was.

'Not bad.'

My mind then went into a sort of panic and, usually full of questions, suddenly I couldn't think of a single word to say. We walked out of the airport in silence.

Halfway to the car I had a brainwave.

'So, what do you do in Australia, mate?' I asked.

He replied, 'I work in the mines.'

A five-word reply. Five words! That was much better than the previous two-word replies. I thought to myself, 'You're getting somewhere, Tom! Good on ya!'

'Wow! What's it like working in the mines?'

'Not bad.'

Damn it. Back down to two-word replies.

You know that saying, 'If you don't have anything nice to say, don't say anything at all'? Well, I live by the saying, 'If you've got nothing to say, just fill the silence with needless words.'

As a result, I found myself starting to narrate everything I was doing. 'Just gonna wind down the window,' I said. 'Now, where's that ticket? There it is. Okay, I'm just gonna slide the ticket into the machine. And look at that – the gate is lifting up! Okay, I'm just going to accelerate forward.' And so on and so on. Needless, inane words.

Now, the thing about a lavender Honda Jazz is that if you don't hit a hill at speed, you'll find yourself going down to first gear and crawling up the gradient at 10 kilometres an hour. I'm not sure if you're aware but the Coromandel would have to have some of the worst roads in the world – winding, so steep, extremely vomit-inducing. We used to go there for holidays in my youth and I'm still processing the trauma of those car trips and the resulting motion sickness.

Anyway, there I was, after an hour of silence, still trying to think of conversation topics, not having realised we'd reached the windiest, steepest hill on our route. Almost instantly I had to go down to first gear. We were crawling up those hills at an embarrassing rate when one of those big trucks carrying logs came up behind me. It tooted for me to get into the slow vehicle bay.

As it thundered past, I thought to myself, 'You have reached a new low, Sainsbury.'

We were about an hour from reaching our destination, and I was scraping the bottom of the barrel for conversation topics, so I just came out with the question, 'What are your thoughts on Syria?'

'Who's she?' came his reply.

Now, you may laugh, but I suddenly had an 'in'. He had finally asked *me* a question!

I spent the next five minutes talking about a topic I didn't know very much about. That topic managed to fill five minutes of silence, so that was good.

When we finally reached the beach house, I was thinking to myself, 'Now he's somebody else's problem'.

He got out of the lavender Honda Jazz and sauntered over to some of the other dudes at the house. They cracked open a beer for him and he chatted away like nobody's business. I was shellshocked. How could I have held so little interest that he couldn't talk to me like that?

I guess the moral of the story is Bad Conversationalist Kiwis just might not have anything to talk about with certain people but can be quite at home shooting the breeze with people of a like mind.

The worst thing about the whole story, though, was later that night, when everyone was drunk, Katy Perry started playing on the UE Boom and our hero, the Bad Conversationalist, knew every lyric to every goddamn song! Goddamn it. If only I'd known! We could've sung together the whole way ...

THE FAMILY UNIT

Whether we like it or not, our families make an indelible mark on who we are – and it's the luck of the draw who we end up with. Our family members can either be absolute angels or absolute rotters, and it's completely out of our control. Unless you believe in Buddhism ... Anyway, let's meet the members of the Kiwi family unit – the good, the bad and the oh-so ugly.

MODERN MUMS

It starts off bad and gets worse. There's this burning desire inside some women to have children, but then there's a fertility issue. 'We've been trying for two years now,' they say. This statement has an adverse effect on anyone who hears it, as it causes them to visualise the couple doing the 'trying'. And then there's the fertility treatment if things haven't been easy. All their friends are getting pregnant no problem at all, and finally they do. Then there's the briefest of times as they walk around with a glow, finally achieving what they wanted so badly.

At three months, they're allowed to share the news because they're through the touch-and-go stage. And they bathe in the warmth of all the compliments. Except when they're dealing with the sickness of varying degrees. Sometimes they're bedridden. Sometimes they're diagnosed with gestational diabetes. Regardless, they're always on edge about the health of the baby, constantly googling various syndromes it may end up having.

The birth is just around the corner and they shuffle along with their varicose veins and heartburn until the due date flies by. That means everyone is on pause, quietly begrudging them for not hurrying up and delivering. The various grandmothers involved are absolutely desperate to get their hands on that baby. As are various strangers, who place their hands on a pregnant belly like it's public property. Everyone has an opinion, and everyone has their own birthing story about how horrendous it is.

When the labour is finally induced, agony follows. Any plans for a home birth are thrown out the window as the Modern Mum-to-be is rushed to hospital. After 30 hours of tearing, screaming and mucus, a wet, mewling monster is placed on the euphoric mother and, in seconds, the various grandmothers appear full of advice (for her) and congratulations (for him) like he actually had anything to do with it.

At this point, everything kicks into a new gear. The baby barely sleeps. The mastitis kicks in. The baby is underweight and the Plunket nurse is no help. The father goes back to work after two weeks and our heroines are plunged into a completely new routine whilst their friends, who only visit occasionally, appear online to be living a life of bliss. This causes depressive thoughts to creep in, and the chronic lack of sleep completely demoralises her. There's so much love for the wee thing. But it's hard. My god, it's hard. It's terrible.

The wee one grows ... but still doesn't sleep. The simple task of finishing a cup of coffee is nigh on impossible, so it requires constant reheating in the microwave. It's also nigh on impossible to go to the bathroom without having the baby scream bloody murder at your absence. Just managing one thing a day, like going to the supermarket, is a miracle. And the washing. Constant washing. Washing was bad before but now it's something else.

Next minute, they're toddlers and everything has to be child-proofed. At this stage, they get into everything and will cry at a moment's notice. Strange sicknesses are constantly afflicting them, and it's never just mild sicknesses. They always have huge temperatures and are being raced to hospital in the middle of the night as everyone prays they don't die. They monopolise everyone's time. Our Modern Mum can't focus on anything for more than a minute without their child having an accident or pulling some sort of attention-seeking stunt. Oh, and there's the tantrums … and the occasional hitting as their precious little one learns the boundaries of what it means to be a human and what they can achieve with the might of their emotions.

Then there's the coffee groups, which are a great idea – mothers with children of a similar age all getting together and supporting one another. But then come the comparisons. 'Oh, Braxton isn't holding his head up yet? Oh, well I'm sure it'll be okay. My Lola has been holding her head up since she was a week old, but we all knew she was advanced.'

It's about this time when people start to ask whether the beleaguered parents will have more of them. It seems unfair to have only the one child, but she just can't put herself through that labour again … not to mention those first six weeks. People say you'll forget those first six weeks. Eventually they do forget them and have another child.

Modern Mum's school friend Felicity is onto her fourth boy, which leads to question marks around her motives and morality. Surely four children is excessive in this day and age?

Once there's multiple children, they're referred to as 'Miss Four' and 'Mister Two'. They delight everyone with the quirky things they say to each other as if they are the most unique, hilarious creatures that have ever come into existence, and all the while they're completely unaware their audience's eyes are glazing over.

Every prospective parent has that gamble in the back of their mind. Will this be a lovely child? Or will they be absolutely horrible? Will they be a serial killer? Will they hate me?

They *will* hate you.

They become teenagers before anyone even realises it, and they hate their parents, who are now their worst enemies. Even so, when they leave home, it's physically painful. They don't ring up nearly as much as their parents would like them to, and when they do ring up, it's to ask for money, or for their Modern Mum to come and do their washing.

When they reach adulthood and seem to be settling down with someone and just might have some children of their own, suddenly a desperation fills our heroine. She can't express the desperation too much in case she comes off as pushy, so she'll distance herself from her child, hoping that when the next generation of babies arrives, she'll be able to throw herself into the very vulnerable position of loving it with all her might even though she knows how much can go wrong.

I mean, yes, people talk about the benefits, and how they love something so much. But it seems like hell. I guess someone has to do it.

THE EASY-GOING DAD

As a gross generalisation, I would say women get more complicated as they hit middle age, whilst men get far less complicated. It seems that all middle-aged dads focus on is a leisure activity of choice – fishing/golf/yachting – their job, in which they're at the top of their game, and their family. Very little else concerns them. I call this breed of person the Easy-going Dad.

The Easy-going Dad is unflappable when disaster strikes. Got a flat tyre on the motorway at 3 am? No problem. The Easy-going Dad will come help you without any discernible annoyance, even though he's had to drive two hours to get to you. He'll tell you it's no bother and take the opportunity to teach you how to change a tyre.

Found yourself plunged into financial hardship, owing a loan shark $30,000, with the threat of losing toes if you don't pay up? The Easy-going Dad will take it all in his stride. He'll calm you down and cast absolutely no judgement about your horrendous financial skills. He'll then come up with a comprehensive plan of how to pay the money back.

The Easy-going Dad is so very proud whenever a member of his family succeeds. If his child manages to get a degree in basket weaving, he'll be there beaming with pride as his son collects his certificate. He and his wife will happily stand on either side of their recently graduated offspring, who is in his formal shirt and tie, and they'll smile for the obligatory photo.

Oh and the Easy-going Dad just loves visiting his adult child's flat or new house. He loves to check everything out whilst noting where he could do some handiwork. He even readily volunteers for painting.

If you've bought a new fixture, say a coffee table or a bookshelf, which he approves of, he'll comment about it at least five times.

'Yeah, that's really good having that shelf there. You can just come in and put your keys on it. Maybe if you put a couple of hooks under there, you'd be able to hang your coats or scarves. I can pop around next Sunday, if that suits, and put the hooks in for ya.'

The Easy-going Dad is usually the slowest within a group. By that I mean his wife or children will be talking and will have moved through a further three conversation topics before Easy-going Dad pipes up with his ponderings on the subject that has been occupying his mind whilst everyone else has moved on.

'I just think that if you get the kids out playing rugby, then this obesity epidemic will be stopped in its track,' he'll say.

I've met many of these fellows in my time, but it wasn't until I met my twentieth (or so) that I decided to work out if he was actually as easy-going as he portrayed himself to be. I wanted to work out if there was anything that rubbed him up the wrong way.

At a small social gathering, he was standing there wearing a T-shirt that strained over his stomach. His short and knobbly legs led down to a jandaled foot. His curly hair was thinning, but he had chosen not to cut it short, so you could just see snippets of scalp. His ear canals were home to a wealth of hair. He was sporting a sunburn because he had been out fishing on the gulf. He hadn't managed to catch any fish, but he was just happy to spend the day with his wife.

Meanwhile, she was hurrying around the kitchen, in a sarong and red lippy, really stressing about the news that her second (and absent) daughter had started going to therapy.

'She'll probably blame me for everything,' she frets.

I don't take up his offer of the seat he is sitting in, but he insists. He moves to an uncomfortable fold-out chair. I politely sip his proffered beer. He is, I believe, 12 beers down.

I ask him if anything annoys him. He ponders for a moment then tells me he sometimes gets road rage. I think that's a blanket answer that everyone has to that question, so it's void.

I ask if there is anything else. He really ponders the question, behaving like the answer will be a precious gift for me. But he struggles.

I ask him if there's anything that would make him angry. Someone doing something to his family, he says. He then says he can't imagine it would be much fun being in a concentration camp.

Later, I ask him if he has any vices. He says he likes beer and maybe has a few too many of those of a weekend. But he's a pleasant drunk, so I give him a pass.

He then scans his brain. 'Vices ...' he says under his breath. 'Vices ... I might have to get back to you on that one.'

And he does get back to me. More than a year later, he sidles up to me and says, 'I've been thinking about your question.'

I scan my brain. Even when he narrows it down to my question about his vices, I still can't remember the conversation clearly – but I pretend I do.

He tells me that whenever there's a Wendy's around he just can't help getting himself a Flake milkshake.

'How often do you go past a Wendy's?' I ask him.

'Christmas shopping,' he said. 'And getting the wife a present I sometimes go into the mall.'

Twice a year, he indulges his vice of a Wendy's Flake Shake.

MOTHER/DAUGHTER BEST FRIENDS

There seems to be a few mother/adult daughter relationships out there that are a bit on the tense side. I've witnessed the occasional adult daughter roll her eyes when her mother speaks and, in turn, I've witnessed the mother roll her eyes when her daughter speaks. But then there are the Mother/Daughter Best Friends.

I've observed a couple of these in my time. My first and favourite was a mother/daughter courier team in Matamata. During my pre-teen years I studied them from afar. They both wore pancake foundation with rouge and blue eyeshadow, and both had peroxided hair teased to within an inch of its life. The only differentiating quality between the two women was that the mother was somewhat heavier.

I would often see mother and daughter driving around in their courier van, chatting away. Mother would always drive, and daughter would do the mad dash from the van to make their deliveries. It seemed to be a great set-up.

When I got older and went to the local bars (underage), I would see mother and daughter there wearing similar clothing to each other and chatting away. They were both fans of light blue jeans, tapered, with a collared polo shirt or a tucked-in rugby shirt, and pointed-toe boots. The polo shirts would be your pinks, your baby blues, or the local rugby team's colours. Their 'going out' clothing was similar to their work clothes in the sense that their courier uniforms consisted of a collared polo shirt with black tapered jeans and pointed-toe boots.

A few months into my character study, I started to notice a fella sniffing around the daughter – in the romantic sense. He was a weedy man with a missing front tooth. He worked at the plumbing store and I presumed they had first connected when the daughter dropped a parcel off to him at work. Apparently, this gentleman knew my father.

During the lead-up to Christmas, my father visited the plumbing store, with me in tow, and this gentleman was ogling a female client – another peroxide-blonde wearing pale-blue tapered denims. He leaned over the counter and said to my father, 'If I was Santa Claus, I'd ask her to sit on my lap and we'd talk about the first thing that popped up.' This was followed by two quick pump-ups of his eyebrows. My father chuckled along politely.

Anyway, this plumbing-store salesman and the courier got together, which drove a huge wedge between her and her mother. Daughter moved out of home and next time I saw the mother she was in her courier van all alone, having to park the van and laboriously get out to make the deliveries. This must've slowed down her productivity considerably. The daughter then took the drastic measure of dying her hair chestnut (though still teased).

But it wasn't to last. The plumbing-store salesman apparently 'did the dirty' on his new girlfriend. The daughter went crawling back to her mother. Next time I saw mother and daughter together they were in the van chatting away animatedly as if that little blip had never happened.

I actually saw them years later at a concert in New Plymouth. For some reason, they were in the VIP booths, dancing away. I looked up at them from the stalls and was shocked by this blast from the past. By then, the daughter looked exactly how I remembered the mother, and the mother looked like a grey-haired (though still teased) granny.

I checked in on them later to see if they were still having the time of their lives, and they were – it was a U2 concert after all. However, another woman had joined them. This addition was someone I can only deduce was the daughter's daughter, so there were three generations of best friends! Unfortunately, the granddaughter didn't have frizzy hair. She'd gone for a peroxide blonde, but sadly it was dead straight.

Another set of Mother/Daughter Best Friends I observed was only through a fleeting, tantalising, eavesdropping snippet. They were at the Viaduct in Auckland. Both were tanned. The mother had very glossy, long, blonde hair and her daughter had very glossy black hair, but essentially in the same style. They both had singlets on and seemed to be proud of their tanned, shapely arms. I want to say the mother was 50 and the daughter was maybe 28. They also both had French-tipped nails. They were drinking white wine and had some sort of crumbed calamari number for their bar snack.

I sat as close as I could to listen in on their conversation without them realising it. The conversation was very frank. The daughter was complaining about her man. She was telling her mother that she was more than ready to give him oral pleasure, but he never wanted to reciprocate. The mother nodded without any judgement, but she didn't have any advice either.

Later, the mother asked her what car her daughter's man was driving these days. He was driving a Polestar apparently, to which the mother responded, 'Very nice.'

Their meals of mussels arrived, and they talked about the latest diets they were trying. The mother then asked if the daughter thought her man was being faithful. The daughter shrugged and said she hoped so, then showed her mother the earrings he had bought her. The mother was very impressed and asked how much they cost. (Side note: the mother's favourite gesture seemed to be taking her long blonde hair and throwing it over her shoulder.)

Later, a gentleman joined them. He must've been over 70. I want to say late seventies. He was very well dressed, very tanned, and had obviously had a facelift somewhere along the way. He kissed the mother on the lips and then she introduced the man to her daughter. He kissed her a little feebly, trying to cover his protruding veneers with his lips. He then proceeded to give both mother and daughter gifts – matching necklaces, which both women cooed over. The interloper then led the mother and daughter out of the restaurant and into the throngs of people. I felt I'd garnered a lot of information about these women in a very short time – and I loved them dearly for it.

THE DOCILE GIRLFRIEND/WIFE

There was this girl at my small-town high school, let's call her Christine, every detail of whose existence was dictated by her boyfriend. She was a serial monogamist from age 10. When she got into a relationship, she would take on every aspect of her boyfriend. I became friends with her during her only window of singledom, when she was 15. She was fantastic – funny, smart, clever, witty, all the good things – then she got into a relationship and everything changed. Let's call her boyfriend Ben. He was a lovely guy as well. But together, they were insufferable.

Public displays of affection were commonplace for them. They were forever making out in front of us, and heaven forbid if you ended up staying the night after a party and had to sleep in the same room as them. They'd freely have sex mere metres away from your sleeping bag – and the sex sounded limp. All whimpers and raw emotionality. 'I love you so much, baby' was always whispered mid-climax.

At one stage, Ben went away to an athletics camp for three days. We were all excited that we'd get the old, fun Christine back. But all we got was a Misery Guts (another species of New Zealander we'll come across soon).

She'd arrive at school with a sour look on her face. When anyone asked if she was okay, she'd always reply, 'I just really miss Ben.'

At random times throughout the day, she'd say, 'I wonder what Ben's up to now ...'

During those three days, they'd talk every night on the phone for three hours. Three hours?! What on earth is there to talk about for that long?

They were always having fights too. When his mates were playing rugby on the field, Ben would want to join them, but he had Christine hanging off him. Eventually, he'd extricate himself and join the boys. This miffed Christine, so she'd guilt-trip him, which always ended in them having a big talk and her running away, crying.

Her tears would continue into class. Everyone relished the drama and would ask her what was wrong. This resulted in her running out of the room. Her two best girlfriends, who loved the drama the most, would run out and console her. Meanwhile, Ben would feel so guilty, he'd go out and talk to her.

We'd all watch the whole exchange through the classroom window because, of course, the whole exchange had to happen right outside the window. After a few minutes, they'd make up with an overly passionate kiss and everything would be all right again. So much so that that night, at a party, they'd have whimpering sex in your parents' bed without your knowledge.

Later in life, I became friends with a woman we'll call Gemma. She was in a long-term relationship with someone we'll call Gavin. More than anything else, Gemma used to say: 'Gavin would love that,' 'I'd love to come but I'll just check with Gavin if I can,' and 'Gavin hasn't texted me for the last hour, I hope everything is okay.'

Gavin was a complete dickhead. Everyone thought so. He was obnoxious, misogynistic, homophobic, racist and was always complaining about 'dole-bludgers' even though he didn't know any personally. Meanwhile, Gemma was lovely.

Their relationship was kinda textbook emotionally abusive, but we didn't know that at the time. Gemma was completely enthralled by Gavin. They did have a wee break-up at one stage. She told a group of us at a rehearsal, then burst out crying. As she fell onto a friend's shoulder, we all shared a gleeful glance. Thank god we'd never have to see Gavin again!

After rehearsal we took Gemma out to get boozed. She cried so much that I let loose about my true feelings for Gavin. I regretted it, though, when I found out they got back together that very night. Apparently, he sent her a message saying he couldn't live without her and she went running back.

When they got engaged, a designated friend took her aside one night and tactfully told her not to go through with the wedding. She didn't listen. They got married and are still together now. He loves to sit in the jacuzzi after work and she loves getting his beer and snacks for him. And I can imagine this little scenario is how it'll play out for them for the rest of their lives.

When I was a child, I was friends with the son of a battery-chicken farmer. Our friendship eventually ended because I kept teasing him that he was romantically involved with his sister. I don't know why I found that idea so funny or why I continuously teased him about it. In hindsight, I completely appreciate being ditched because I had been a complete shit.

During the window of our friendship, I visited his home a few times. This was an opportunity for me to witness his family dynamics. His father was a big, zany personality, always telling jokes and always with a smile on his face. His mother, on the other hand, was a complete non-personality, who only wore beige or mushroom cardigans, barely spoke above a whisper and did everything for her family with a worried look in her eyes.

Even though she did everything for her family, they completely took advantage of her and were terribly rude. I witnessed the said incestuous sister yelling abuse at her mother and her mother giving no fight back. She just looked at her child with her worried eyes and a smile/grimace on her face. The reason for the yelling? Apparently, the timid mother had extended the hem of her daughter's uniform to regulation length and the daughter didn't like it.

At dinnertime, the mother would behave like a maid. None of us would move as she ran around the table, serving the food then later collecting the plates, avoiding eye contact and not making a fuss.

Obviously, I didn't see her son after I was ditched for my incest gag, but many years later I ran into the daughter, who didn't recognise me. I explained who I was and asked how her parents were. Well, get this! As soon as the kids were old enough, the mother packed her bags and disappeared. She dyed her hair blue and was living with her cousin in Taranaki. Meanwhile, the father had a breakdown and – according to his daughter – was now dating someone twice his age. Given he must've been in his early fifties at that point, his new girlfriend would have been over 100. Isn't that all just wonderful?

THE KNOW-IT-ALL DAD

I have a friend whose father works in 'finance' in Tauranga. Let's call this guy Bruce. Even though Bruce works in the finance sector, he feels confident enough to give career advice to anyone in any field.

This is an example of a conversation I overheard: 'You work in landscaping, do ya? There must be a bit of competition in that. What you need to do is get your head above everyone else. You got a good logo? You need a good logo. What you need is a point of difference. Do you have an arborist on your team? No? Well, you need to get one. That'll be your point of difference. Everyone will hire you then. You can thank me later.' All of which was followed with a knowing wink.

I asked his son, my friend, how his father knew about the landscaping industry. My friend told me Bruce had no expertise in the landscaping field. He was simply making assumptions.

Bruce would then sidle up to me. 'You work in the arts, do ya? Can't be much money in that. What you need to do is get yourself a website. Get some nice photos of yourself and put them on it. Because you're selling yourself essentially. You put on shows, do ya? What you need to do is do a deal with a restaurant. Charge people for a full meal and they'll get entertainment at the same time. You can charge an arm and a leg for it. That's what you need to do. Make it a real evening. You can thank me later for that advice, son.' Then came the knowing wink.

I asked his son, my friend, if Bruce had a side gig as a showbiz agent or something. But, no, he didn't. He just wanted to give advice on a topic he didn't know much about. He was a quintessential Kiwi Know-it-all Dad.

Whenever a conversation took place, no matter the topic, Bruce always knew best. Being in the same room as him whilst the television was on was very entertaining.

'He calls himself a chef? I could cook circles around him.'

'What the hell is that ref doing? They should've asked me to be the ref. At least I know the bloody rules.'

'Why is she wearing that? It's distracting. I could've got her into something much better than that.'

Bruce was also an expert on every element of running the country. 'Those bloody assholes in the Beehive know nothing. They should come and ask me for advice. I'll sort out the economy/housing crisis/poverty/pollution/international affairs/Treaty of Waitangi.'

I soon discovered he never admitted to not knowing something. If I mentioned a celebrity, or a current event, or a rule of physics, I'd check in to see if Bruce knew what I was talking about.

He'd say, 'Yes I do, but can you just remind me of it?'

I'd explain who/what/when it was and he'd say, 'Yes, yes, yes, yes. I know exactly what you're talking about.'

Bruce was a keen writer of letters to the editor. I had no idea about this until his son, my friend, told me. I made a habit of checking the newspaper after that and there he'd be, rabbiting on, giving advice on all manner of things. This is how Air New Zealand should conduct themselves … This is how you solve a gambling addiction … This is how you get people to stop being depressed …

He wrote two books during the time I knew him. They were his personal musings on what was written in the Bible and the Quran.

'Here ya go,' he said, dumping a huge manuscript on the table in front of me. 'Here are my thoughts on Mohammed and the whole damned business.'

I'm talking at least 800 pages of his writing. He was handing it to me like I was very lucky to be able to read it. It was like he thought I'd readily pause everything else going on in my life so I could enthusiastically read this new gospel.

I read through the first 10 pages then pretended to have read the rest. Those 10 pages were basically him explaining how his life philosophies were better thought out than what was in the Quran.

He was very keen to get these two books published. Before sending them to the top publishing houses, he asked a friend to do a quick edit on them (even though he assumed it would just be a few typos here and there).

The friend came back with some serious suggestions. He included a series of questions querying whether there were a market for such a genre of book. This sent our Bruce into an absolute rage. He talked himself into thinking this editing friend didn't know what the hell he was talking about. He was a charlatan, an idiot. Bruce knew what was being published these days and knew there was a market for random guys' thoughts on religion, so he didn't do any of the suggested edits.

His covering letter to the publishing house, which I read many years later, basically patronised the publishing houses because he knew more about publishing and what people were reading than they did. The books weren't published.

Next time I saw Bruce, though, he was very chipper about the whole thing. He shrugged, saying the publishers didn't know a bestseller when they saw one, and it was no wonder the publishing industry was dying when no one was taking such calculated risks.

I did discover one subject he wasn't completely clued up on, though – and I found it surprising. His son, my friend, and I were driving out west when his car broke down. We didn't know what the hell was going on. Being quite poor at the time, we didn't want to have to call AA, so we called Bruce for advice.

We put him on speakerphone so that we could tinker with the motor as he spoke. He listened to what the problem was then said he had no idea how to fix it and that we should call AA. With that, he hung up. My friend and I stared at each other, not able to comprehend that his father hadn't at least claimed to know about something.

THE MARTYR MOTHER

My mother is an absolute blessing, so I've never experienced the Martyr Mother first-hand. But I have observed it in quite a few others. This is the kind of shit they say: 'I wish I could go to the movies today like you guys are doing, but somebody has to stay here and clean up the breakfast dishes.' Then they'll shrug and everyone else will feel terrible, which seems to be what they'd been aiming to achieve all along.

Guilt-tripping is the Martyr Mother's most frequently used tool. They love little snide comments. They say shit like: 'Well, I'm glad *she's* having fun', and 'Lucky for some, I guess,' and 'We can't all go and follow our dreams. Some of us have to be practical.'

Listening to these women, you might assume they're terribly hard done by. You might think they've had to sacrifice a lot. And you might think they're miserable victims of circumstance. But don't be fooled – it's all of their own choosing. They could easily go to the movies and leave the breakfast clean-up for later, but they choose not to because they love the power that being a martyr provides.

In my early teenage years, I spent a week with one such mother. Her son was an acquaintance (not so much a friend) and he invited me along on a beach holiday. Now, the son constantly made me laugh with his goofy sense of humour, but he also had terrible BO. Everyone at school talked about it behind his back. These days, I would have the maturity to just subtly tell him. But back then, I just went with it, desperately taking shallow breathes through my mouth whenever I was in close proximity to him.

I was dropped off at their house at the start of the holidays. It was a very hot, dry summer so the son was particularly pungent. He was also suffering unfortunate acne at the time. The father was quietly finishing packing the car out the front of the house. Because they had four children, and a conventional car could transport three, they had bought a people mover – a sort of white van thing with electronic sliding doors on the side.

The Martyr Mother was on the phone talking to a friend about another friend. 'Well, she only had the one child, so she doesn't know how easy it is for her. She has no idea. I wish I could just up and leave for the Gold Coast, but some of us have four children and a mortgage.'

When she hung up, she looked me over. Seeing me definitely didn't fill her with joy. There was irritation and also a sense of disdain over how I conducted myself. The previous time I'd seen her, she'd told me her son was picky to feed but cheap because he didn't eat much. Whereas, she said, my mother was lucky because I wasn't a picky eater, but I must have been expensive to feed because of the quantities I consumed. Now listen, if that wasn't a backhanded compliment, I don't know what is.

At that moment ol' BO Boy emerged from the hall, with fuzzy hair and a smooshed pillow face.

'Good afternoon,' his mother said. It was 10 am. 'I'd started to think you must've thought we were going tomorrow.'

With that, she headed into the kitchen, shrugging. 'God, I would love to have been able to sleep in, but someone has to pack the groceries for the week.'

The car ride was hell. It was a two-hour trip and anything anyone said was heard by everyone else. I foolishly mentioned that my brother had gone on a school trip to Europe that year, to which the Martyr Mother replied, 'God, I'd love to be able to go to Europe. I can't see it happening any time soon, though. Far too much to do here.'

At the beginning of the week, whenever I'd finish a meal, she would say, 'Goodness, you finished that quickly. You must've been starving.'

I then tried a new tactic of not eating everything, to which she'd respond: 'Didn't you like it?'

'No, I thought it was lovely.'

'If you want me to make you something else, I can.'

'No, no, no, I'll eat it.'

And then I'd eat it and she'd say, 'Your mother is so lucky that you aren't picky. Must be expensive to feed you though, with the quantities you eat.'

Let's just say I've never been happier than when that week at the beach was over.

I drifted away from her son pretty quickly after school, but towards the end of our time together he got his BO under control. In fact, he swung too far the other way. He was forever coating himself in Lynx deodorant. At every opportunity, it would come out and be sprayed everywhere, threatening to kill us all by butanol poisoning.

Many years later, I ran into his mother at a wedding, strangely, in Auckland. It was a complete surprise to see her there. She had grey hair and more of a stoop, but otherwise she hadn't changed. The first thing she said on seeing me was, 'Gosh, you've really filled out.'

I didn't even flinch at that and simply asked after her son. She told me what she knew about his life. He had left for Europe as soon as he could – Spain, actually. Literally the absolute opposite side of the world. It would be harder for him to get further away unless he was an astronaut. Last time she'd heard, he'd had two girlfriends on the go. But he was useless at communicating. She then said, 'Lucky for some to be gallivanting around the world, isn't it?'

I asked her if she'd thought about going over to visit him.

'God, no, the other kids couldn't cope without me being around to babysit the grandkids. And we've got the business. You know, some of us have to stay behind and do the boring things to keep the economy going.'

I nodded and excused myself for the bathroom, which wasn't needed, but I definitely needed to get away from that energy!

BABY BOOMER PARENTS

I mean, look, intergenerational tension has been around forever, and I could say a lot of negative things about the Baby Boomers, but I won't. For example, I could say that they have ruined the property market, that they assume the younger generation are whingers even though society is definitely harder to navigate these days, and I could say that they've ruined the environment and the world their children, grandchildren and great-grandchildren will have to attempt living in. But I'm not even going to touch on any of that, let alone mention it.

What I love most about the Baby Boomer generation is how personable they can be. The neuroses and social anxiety that seem to be prevalent in the younger generations appear to be absent in these lovelies.

I was visiting a friend's apartment once, in an apartment block where you never interact with any of your neighbours. In this apartment block you'd get into the elevator and if someone else was there you'd avoid eye contact and stand in silence.

Anyway, when I visited the apartment, I found my friend's Baby Boomer Parents were staying for a few days. In that time, they had (with a charming naiveté) befriended everyone in the entire building.

'We were just in the hallway and your neighbours came out. A lovely Chinese woman. Hei, I think her name was. Wasn't it, Grant?'

'I didn't catch her name.'

'It's because you didn't have your hearing aid in. But yes, she moved over from China to finish her study, but ended up staying on because she loves it here so much. She's got a Caucasian boyfriend. So ... (She shrugged in a way I couldn't interpret.) She said she's seen you in the hallway but hasn't talked to you. You should definitely talk to her because, apparently, she's a real whiz in the kitchen. We actually shared a few recipes.'

I also love how Baby Boomers are generous in every aspect (except for maybe allowing other people onto the property market).

'Darling, I've let myself into your flat and filled the fridge with groceries. And Dad's paying for dinner tonight, okay? So, make sure your friends order the crayfish.'

They're also obsessed with the routes from one place to the other.

'Which way did you end up going? Ah, so you bypassed Foxton, did you? That was probably a good idea because I know they were doing roadworks there. How long did it end up taking you? Ah yes, when you return can I suggest you take the Kaupuki turn-off? That'll shave a good ten minutes off I reckon.'

Baby Boomers also tend to be obsessed with the weather.

'We went up to Napier for the weekend to catch up with your mum's friend Jill and her husband, Dick. Anyway, the weather report said it was going to be raining the whole weekend, but the Saturday was absolutely fine. The Sunday there were a few showers, but we could still go out and play golf. And then the Monday was when the rain really set in. What's the weather up your way? Have the rain clouds moved up there?'

Baby Boomers are also obsessed with the concept of grandchildren.

'I ran into Jan Coates at the supermarket. Do you know who I mean when I say Jan Coates? Anyway, her daughter Colleen, was she at school with you? She just gave birth to her fourth son! But he was nine weeks early and apparently it was a horrendous birth. Anyway, she was asking if I had any grandchildren on the horizon and, sadly, I had to tell her that you weren't even in a long-term relationship ...'

What I also appreciate about Baby Boomers is their tendency to enjoy the finer things in life. They're not focused on romantic relationships or work because they've been there, done that. They are now able to pursue their passion for cheese and wine. In fact, there's a whole subset of Baby Boomer men who are obsessed with cheese – and the more pungent the better.

'Try this unpasteurised Rocamadour cheese from the Dordogne,' they'll say. 'It's stinky as hell but, my god, it hits the mark.'

Some Baby Boomers have bucket lists filled with activities they want to complete whilst they're still able. I met a huge group of Bucket-Lister Baby Boomers whilst visiting the Chatham Islands. The group had met through yachting and liked to go on a group excursion once a year. The patriarch of the group was visiting the Chathams solely to experience the local paua and crayfish.

If he found out that you'd had some local paua, he would ask for specific details about how it had been cooked. Then he'd salivate over the details of its texture. His eyes would stare at your lips as if he were imagining you eating that sweet, sweet paua for the first time. The others in the group had brought over various stinky cheeses and loved proffering them with artisanal crackers and dessert grapes.

Two of their group joined us for a trip to Pitt Island, where we were driven along the cliffs, visited an ancient whaling cottage, and then had dinner at the homestead. On the flight back, the Baby Boomers were very disparaging of the meal. 'I mean, those peas were cooked to within an inch of their lives. And don't even start on how dry the mutton was.'

Basically, they couldn't wait to get back to their accommodation and crack open the Clearview chardonnay from the Hawke's Bay and unwrap that blue cheese from Burgundy in the hopes of washing away the horrible aftertaste of such an abysmal lunch (which I had found very satisfactory, maybe even a little tasty).

THE IRRITABLE DAD

There is a breed of father out there who appears to be perpetually pissed off. His tone is always clipped, and his face never shows human warmth. I call this New Zealander the Irritable Dad.

My first dealings with such a man was a friend's father. I bore the full brunt of his irritation when I joined him and his family on a car trip to the beach. He was a tall man, and bald, and he had a huge stomach and thin, white legs. His wife was short and similarly round and was always experimenting with various red hair colours ranging from safety orange to deep auburn. Whereas she was lovely and always ready to laugh, the Irritable Dad never once cracked a smile.

Anyway, there we were in the car and I had the misfortune of being seated behind him. Being a tall man, he had extended the seat as far back as it could go. As a result, I basically had my thighs pressed against my chest.

His driving started off measured but grew more and more erratic as we delved deeper into our two-and-a-half-hour trip. Our conversation also devolved from light and humorous at the beginning to stony silence at the end, as everyone just willed the goddamn nightmare to be over.

What was the nightmare? Well, the Irritable Dad took exception to every single other car on the road. 'Creep,' he'd whisper under his breath whenever one passed us. And if he felt a car was too close behind us, he'd slam on the brakes at various intervals to 'teach them a lesson'.

At one point, I cracked my window open a little, hoping the fresh air would alleviate the nausea that had resulted from his erratic driving.

'Close that, please,' the Irritable Dad said in a monotone voice. 'You'll ruin the air conditioning unit.'

One hour in, the younger child needed to use the bathroom. He softly asked his mother, who passed the information on to the Irritable Dad. He didn't register the request, instead choosing to stare sternly at the road in front of him, his hands tight around the wheel.

'Did you hear that, darling? Joshy needs to use the bathroom.'

Suddenly, without warning, the Irritable Dad jerked the steering wheel to the side and pulled off the road, at full speed, into a rest area. He then sat in the car, not talking, whilst the rest of us went about our business and thanked the lord above for the gift of fresh air.

We got back into the car and as soon as we were back onto the road, I realised I needed to go to the toilet again, but there was no way in hell I was going to tell anyone.

I just want to note that the Irritable Dad's catchphrase was 'What now?', always said with a sigh and a defeated slackening of his shoulders. Whenever one of his children said, 'Dad?', he'd sigh and slacken his shoulders, then say, 'What now?' The tone of the 'What now?' ranged from exhausted annoyance to all-out rage.

The holiday was a lot of fun whenever we were away from the Irritable Dad – and that seemed to make him happy as well. He was often wont to say, 'What are you still doing here? Get lost!' This was our cue to run down to the beach for the day, where we'd get terribly sunburnt.

One morning, I got up before the others and was pretending to do a word puzzle at the dining table when the Irritable Dad scuffed up in his dressing gown.

On seeing me, he sighed and shook his head. He then scuffed into the kitchenette area and switched on the kettle. It did nothing, so he cursed under his breath before picking the kettle up, then putting it back on its stand. 'You bloody thing!'

The taking off and putting back on soon became more frenetic. 'Why don't you bloody … !'

And then there was silence. He sighed then turned the switch on at the wall. The kettle started to boil. He sighed a world-weary sigh, folded his arms and leant against the bench.

The only other thing of note about that holiday was that whenever they would pass a dog, everyone, barring the Irritable Dad, would comment on it.

'Oh my god, so cute!'

'Look at that dog, Mum! He looks like he's laughing.'

It turns out the children were all desperate for a pet dog, but the Irritable Dad was completely against it.

One night during the holiday, I heard him bellow, 'I'm sick of having to tell you we are NOT GETTING A DOG!'

I asked my friend why his father was so against dogs and was told the Irritable Dad had said the dog would be neglected by the kids and it would then be left to him to look after 'the bloody thing'.

Cut to two years later, and the family had got a Golden Labrador named Kenya. The next time I visited them, the Irritable Dad had softened somewhat. I walked into the house and he was seated on the couch watching the footy with Kenya lying across his lap.

Later, he yelled at the family to take Kenya out for her evening walk, but no one replied. Grumbling, he took the dog out himself.

When he returned, I heard him saying in a very high-pitched voice, 'Have you done your weewees, Kenya? That's a girl! Do your weewees ...'

Weewees done, they went back to the couch, where Kenya tried to lick Irritable Dad's face as he read the newspaper. 'Get out of it!' he hissed.

She stopped licking for a moment but was clearly desperate to continue. When the opportunity arose, she licked his face again. He allowed it for a few more moments this time before hissing 'Get out of it!' once more. This time Kenya whined, then lay down, her jaw across his thigh.

THE WORKPLACE KIWI

The majority of New Zealand's population work. Actually, I have no idea about that. Taking into account all the children, the retired, the unemployed – does that mean the majority of New Zealanders actually have jobs? God knows. Well, I'm sure there is a census I could read, but who has time for that?

In any case, a lot of us spend a lot of time at a place of work. And a lot of us have the fortune/misfortune of having to work alongside other people. These 'other people' come in a wonderful array of personality types, so let's meet the workplace Kiwi …

THE MISERY GUTS

Once, I worked with a man you could bet your house on. Every time anyone said something positive, he would say something negative.

'Oh my god, I'm so excited, my wife is pregnant!'

'Have you had all the tests for all the syndromes?'

Or ...

'I finally got my licence!'

'I don't know why you'd want to drive in this city. The other day I drove past a huge accident. Two people died.'

Or, my favourite ...

'I've just got all my results back. Thankfully, I don't have any STDs, so we can all relax!'

'But Tom, STDs can take three months to show a positive result ...' And he just left that hanging in the air. His face wasn't grim because of the subject matter being discussed. It was just grim because it was always just grim.

I don't think he was consciously trying to dash everyone's will to live. That was just how he conducted himself. He was a miserable bastard.

Me and my workmate started calling him Misery Guts behind his back, and that moniker eventually spread around to everyone else. It got to the stage where we'd purposely say something positive and then ... wait ... wait ... waaaaiit ... and then Misery Guts would roll out his shitty attitude, making us all feel suicidal, then someone would mutter, 'There goes Misery Guts, right on cue.'

We all worked for this events company. It was a stressful job, and often things were a bit touch and go. Say, for example, the pastries had tipped over in the back of the van en route to the venue and were unusable. New pastries would have to be organised within an hour. Give Misery Guts the task of arranging replacements and he'd say something like, 'I mean, I'll call them, but I doubt they'll be able to do anything in an hour.' That may very well be the case, Misery Guts, but you've got to at least try!

His phone conversation with the pastry people would go like this: 'You probably won't be able to do this, but we need pastries for an event in an hour … you're going to say no, aren't you? You can do it? Oh, that's weird. Are you sure? You can say "no". Okay then, we'll send someone over to collect them.'

He'd hang up and, without any joy in his voice, he'd tell us he'd managed to organise some replacement pastries.

We'd arrange for someone to go and pick them up and he'd say, 'I doubt she'll be able to get to the bakery and back again before the event begins.'

'We've got to at least try,' we'd tell Misery Guts.

He'd shrug. 'Well, good luck in *this* traffic.'

If an event was outdoors, he was even worse.

'It'll definitely rain today,' he'd say.

'The forecast is sunny all day,' we'd say.

'Yeah, but can you trust the forecast? I wouldn't.'

Throughout the day, he'd walk past muttering, 'Those are definitely rainclouds over there.'

We'd get through the event without rain, and you'd go to Misery Guts and say, 'That went well. The sun held out, which is awesome.'

He'd sigh and say, 'Yeah, but hardly anyone showed up, so I'd hardly call it a success.'

I mean, we laughed about him a lot, but it could also really drag you down – especially if your self-esteem was a bit precarious.

One time, a few months before I left, another co-worker lost her rag at him. He was in charge of organising a last-minute ice sculpture. He was telling everyone he doubted anyone would be able to make an ice sculpture in time when a normally timid, smiley young woman turned on him.

'Just ring them, for god's sake! Why are you always so goddamn negative all the fucking time?! All you ever do is whinge and complain and think nothing is ever going to turn out. I'm sick of it!' And she stormed off.

All Misery Guts said in response was, 'I deserved that.'

Nothing more was ever said on the matter. The ice sculpture couldn't be organised in time, so the table was without one, not that any of the clients gave a shit. They just wanted to get drunk.

After the event, Misery Guts said, 'Well, that went terribly.'

Another Misery Guts I knew was a hypochondriac. He told me he was always sick.

'Always sick?' I asked him. 'Like, all the time?'

'There's always something wrong. Like, I'm always at least twenty-five per cent sick.'

I guess it was true. He was always either at the start of a cold, in the depths of a cold, or coming out of a cold. One time he told me he was on his fourth cold for the season and it was the worst yet. He kept soldiering on, though, coming to work, sniffing and coughing and bringing down everyone's mood.

There was no point in suggesting any remedies for him because 'nothing worked'.

'Bed rest works,' a co-worker told him.

'No, it doesn't,' he replied, without missing a beat.

At one point, he was so sure he had a tumour growing on his stomach he even got me to feel it.

'It's a tumour, right?'

'I'm not sure. Have you been to the doctor?'

'Yes, but they said there's nothing wrong with me. It's just a parcel of fat.'

'Then you're fine!'

'I'm not fine. I'm definitely not.'

And he wasn't fine. He'd been right. It was a tumour – cancerous, but thankfully it was very contained and could be easily removed.

When he told us about it, no one was surprised. It was almost like him getting a tumour made complete sense in the poetry of life. He willed bad things into his life and they came true. But, strangely, there was a lightness to his step as soon as it was diagnosed. I don't know how to describe it, but it was almost like he was happy his misery vibes had been justified.

LAZY KIWIS

There is a breed of New Zealander in the workplace who has managed to wrangle things so they can get away with doing absolutely no work. Usually, they can be found in big organisations, where they can hide amongst the masses. They do feature in smaller organisations, but only in situations where they are left to their own devices. A part of me absolutely admires this sort of person. But another part of me is infuriated by their audacity.

I had one friend whose job allowed her to work at two different desks in wildly different parts of the company. If she wasn't at one desk everyone would assume she was at the other desk. She used this to her advantage. She told me she would clock in at the beginning of her shift then shortly after, she'd walk off with a concerned look on her face, shuffling papers as she went. Then she'd go to the mall or the movies, only returning later in the afternoon with a similarly concerned look on her face and shuffling the same papers. No one ever questioned it.

I, myself, have done many a temp job in my time, and whenever an office job would come up, I would leap at the opportunity. Some of the receptionist jobs required me to answer and forward maybe four phone calls a day, then the rest of the time I was left to my own devices – overusing the coffee machine, photocopying things for my personal use, checking my social media.

Once, I'd just printed off 100 pages of something I'd written on the work computer, which had nothing to do with work. It was a script of some description, and I had basically wasted all morning working on my own things.

As I was stapling them together using the office's staples, I looked up and saw my manager striding towards me. I casually placed the scripts into the drawer beside me and smiled whilst my mind went into overdrive. 'This is it,' I thought. 'The gig is up! I'm going to be fired and I'll have to pay back all my wages.'

Instead, my manager told me how happy she was with the job I'd been doing, and that I was so much better than the person I'd replaced. Then she asked if I would care to have the job permanently. I politely turned her down, thinking, 'Jesus Christ, how useless had the person before me been?'

It was during another temp receptionist gig that I saw the best hoodwinking, yet laziest worker of them all. I was at the company for a month and I noticed her pretty early on.

She was loud, smiley and friendly with all her co-workers. But I never actually saw her doing any work. She definitely painted the picture that she was always busy. She always had this air of being occupied with important things about her.

After two weeks, I decided to spend a day recording the 'work' she actually did. And I was not disappointed. She arrived 35 minutes late, claiming traffic had been a nightmare, then sat down at her desk just as the boss ventured out of his office. He was none the wiser to her tardiness.

He said hello. They had a little bit of a catch-up – at her urging – and she found out all about what his kids had been up to recently. He then returned to his office.

Our heroine headed to the staffroom to make herself a coffee. She chatted with another woman in the staffroom about matters unrelated to work. The other woman eventually excused herself.

Our heroine then walked around the office, leaning over various cubicle dividers and having a good old chinwag with three other people about matters not related to work. She then sat at her desk. When I walked past, I noticed she was on social media.

She left for lunch early, saying she was off to the gym. She told everyone that she needed to do it for her 'mental health', but she'd be back before the hour was up.

She eventually arrived back an hour and a half later. She then used the staff bathrooms to have a shower and get back to a presentable look. That took a good 20 minutes. She then asked if anyone in the office would like a store-bought coffee because she was going to do a coffee run. The taking of the orders took about 15 minutes because she was chatting so much in between. She then went for a coffee run and returned 43 minutes later, claiming the traffic was terrible.

At 2:30 pm, she explained to anyone in hearing distance that it was her week to pick up the kids from school, but after picking them up she'd be working from home for the rest of the day. If anyone needed to get in contact with her, all they had to do was give her a buzz. She'd have her phone with her for the rest of the day.

At 4 pm, I was given the task of calling her because someone couldn't find a file she'd been working on. She didn't answer my calls, nor did she reply to my emails.

To be honest, I'm pretty sure she didn't do a single bit of work, but no one seemed to notice so she got away with it. And I kinda appreciate that.

My admiration for her soon soured, though. After having done no work for the entire time I was there, during my last week she was suddenly given a work task that needed to be done by the end of the day. My god, she made a song and dance about it. She was forever broadcasting how stressed she was. At one point, I had to ask her to sign a farewell card for one of the other workers. She stared at me, incredulously, like how dare I interrupt her when she had so much work to do.

I found out later that she'd actually had all week to do the task, but she had obviously procrastinated doing it.

At 3 pm on the day her task had been completed and emailed off, she cracked open the staffroom beers and wines. She told everyone they all deserved it because of the huge day of work they'd all done, and she didn't do a scrap of work for the rest of the day. God bless this audacious Lazy Kiwi.

SUPERMARKET MANAGERS

Having worked in many supermarkets in my time, I want to discuss the supermarket industry and two specific Kiwi character types that exist within it. First, we'll talk about Middle Managers, then we'll discuss the Top Managers.

In all four supermarkets I worked at there were always two managers in charge of me. And every time this manager duo would come in the same combination. One of the managers would be morbidly obese and live off energy drinks, whilst the other would be a bean pole, like exceptionally skinny, and a smoker. These two wonderfully eccentric personalities were always best friends.

Let me repeat that. This combination of men – one obese and one very skinny – occurred at all four supermarkets I worked in. Four separate times. Four identical duos. Isn't that bonkers?

All eight of these managers seemed to be at the supermarket all the time. I only ever worked part-time, but every time I was there these managers were there, putting boxes of groceries onto trolleys or cleaning up spilt oil in aisle seven.

If I started at 6 am they would already be there, wearing hoodies over their uniforms as they got all the boxes of cereal out before the morning rush. If I worked the night shift, they were there, breaking down cardboard boxes and stacking the cat food cans perfectly along the front of the shelves, creating a pristine, pleasing-to-the-eye masterpiece of symmetry (only for some bitch or bastard to come along and ruin their good work by reaching into the back to get the freshest ones).

It took me a long time to even contemplate these men having lives outside the supermarket, considering they were there all the time. That was until one particular duo told me, whilst stacking the jalapeño corn chips, they had coordinated their lunch breaks so they could drive to the local girls' school as the school day was finishing. There, they'd drink energy drinks, eat rotisserie chicken and cream doughnuts and watch as the girls left the school en masse. I can only imagine what the girls thought of them if they noticed them sitting there watching. I should point out that these men were in their late twenties by this point – and neither of them had a girlfriend.

As well as being pervy, they were always ready to laugh. They took their jobs seriously, of course, but if there was an opportunity for a prank or a bit of goofing off, they'd take it.

The beanpole manager of this duo once had to take some time off work because of a bleeding stomach, which had been brought about by drinking too much Pepsi Max. This left the obese man without his best friend. I sat with him in the staffroom and he told me he had really been inspired by the success of Harry Potter, so he'd started writing his own young adult fantasy series involving magic and an orphan. His, however, was a lot more musically based than Harry Potter. I vaguely remember him mentioning a magical flute being involved. As he continued to discuss his project, I was somewhat put off by the sheer commercialism of the venture. Essentially, he just wanted to be a billionaire. That said, it was pleasing to know he had such grand ambitions.

Years after I'd quit working at that supermarket I went back and found them still there, flirting with the schoolgirls who worked at the checkout after school, and cleaning up spilt oil in aisle seven. They were really happy to see me, although I could sense some tension between them.

After a bit of discussion, I found out that the beanpole manager had been promoted from grocery manager to store manager, whilst his obese friend had stayed put in grocery. They were no longer equals, and it was taking its toll on their relationship.

In short, you can identify a supermarket Middle Manager by their 16-hour-plus days, their fondness of energy drinks and other empty-calorie food, their readiness for a laugh and their horny slash somewhat creepy demeanour.

Now let's discuss the Top Managers. My first supermarket job was at a New World and the married couple who ran it were both under five-foot-three. Let's call them Jenny and Mark. They were obsessed with winning the award for top New World of the year. This meant they were forever berating their staff for not having everything perfect in case a secret shopper came around.

They would stride into the supermarket at any time of the day, loudly greeting their regular customers by name. One 'Gidday, Tanya! How are ya?' and suddenly the staff would be on edge. It got so bad for me that one time I heard them come in screaming 'G'day, Cath! How are ya?!' and my entire body was suddenly covered in pins and needles. Had I had a heart attack? No, it was just a garden-variety panic attack. Talking with the other staff I realised we all felt like that. This hobbit duo put us all on edge.

We always won the inter-New World competition, though. And we got five cents extra for every hour we worked in the week leading up to the secret shopper's visit.

Many years later I became involved with a workers' union after they'd approached me with an idea for a Snapchat video they wanted to share to help bring about social change. They told me that the majority of people on the New Zealand rich list were supermarket owners, and these supermarket owners refused to pay their staff the minimum wage. Apparently, they also embarked upon a variety of other evil acts, all whilst buying multiple yachts and – in a wonderful display of nepotism – training their sons up to take over their own supermarkets one day.

One day, as research for the video, I scoped out one of these guys by popping into the supermarket and watching as he walked around fixing up the price tags on the various packaged meats. He seemed pleasant enough and had a friendly demeanour as he answered customers' questions. I had been following him around for about five minutes, keeping at a safe distance, when he noticed me. I made myself look very interested in the crushed garlic selection then hastily made my way out, passing the checkout operators working for less than the minimum wage. The experience left me pondering how he could justify the way he conducted his business when he seemed to be such a normal, approachable dude.

I still did a merciless parody of him – in his carpark and then in his fruit section. I doubt it had any effect, though. If he even noticed it, he probably scoffed and then swam around in his pool filled not with water but with dollar bills.

APOLOGISTS FOR EXISTING

There are New Zealanders out there who are terribly sorry for even existing. These people often begin statements with one of the following:

1. 'I'm so sorry for bothering you, but …'
2. 'Totally feel free to say no, but …'

3. 'I'm such a useless piece of shit. I can't believe I have the audacity to ask anything of you, but …'

What follows these statements are usually terribly innocuous queries. One example: 'I'm so sorry for bothering you, but would you mind possibly moving your car because you've blocked me in and I can't quite squeeze out of the driveway. I'm so sorry to be asking you to do this. If only I had parked on the road today, then I wouldn't need to bother you. If it's too much bother to move your car I totally understand. I'm sure I can just call a taxi. I'll do that now. I'll call a taxi right now. I'm so sorry for bothering you. Carry on doing what is obviously much more important than listening to a stupid piece of shit like me rabbiting on about nothing. I'm so sorry for bothering you. Sorry.'

Sure, I might be exaggerating, but only slightly. There are people like this out there, and I call them Apologists for Existing.

At university I ran across a female version of the species. Let's call her Charlotte. We worked together on a group project for an anthropology paper. Somehow, she was chosen as group leader. This was probably because the rest of us were too lazy to volunteer. She would regularly send emails containing far too many words. The emails would consist of copious apologies that you'd have to wade through to find out what she was actually asking of you. Then she'd undercut her requests by offering to do the task herself before thanking you for bothering to read the email then apologising for taking up too much of your precious time.

My individual task within the project was to write about inherent bias in a newspaper article about Rastafarians. I did it and sent it through to Charlotte. I got a reply email from her at 3 am. The first three sentences were her apologising for even sending me an email when she was sure I had better things to do than read it. She then explained that she had found some grammatical errors in my writing. Would it be okay if she corrected them? But absolutely no worries if not. If I didn't want them to be corrected, she would be totally fine with us submitting the project with them still in it. I replied that of course she could fix the grammatical errors.

As the pressure of the project increased, another student in the group spoke up. He told Charlotte to stop apologising all the time, to be more concise with what she wanted from us, and that none of us took it personally when she asked us to do something or required us to change anything. She nodded whilst flushing bright red, but took on the feedback.

At the time, I thought him doing this was a great idea. But it kinda backfired. What Charlotte started doing was apologising and then instantly apologising for apologising.

'Hi guys, sorry for having to ... shit, sorry. I just said sorry. Sorry for saying sorry. Sorry. Shit ... I'll shut up. Sorry.'

We submitted the group project on time. It was only when I saw the final product that I realised she had done the majority of the work required all by herself. At our next lecture, I managed to weasel out of her that she'd had to do two all-nighters to get all of the work done. This fact made me feel absolutely terrible, but Charlotte simply shrugged off my apologies.

About 10 years later, I ran into Charlotte on Lambton Quay in Wellington. She seemed to have got even worse. Her chest had kinda caved in on itself and her eyes were too furtive and nervous to meet mine. She saw me first and did a quick wave. She then instantly seemed to regret getting my attention.

The first thing she said was sorry for breaking my concentration. She then apologised for making me late for some important meeting I probably had to attend. I assured her there was no such meeting and suggested perhaps we could grab a coffee because I had an hour to kill. This concept seemed to terrify her, but we went to a cafe where she apologised to the barista as she ordered a cup of tea. Apparently, caffeine made her too anxious.

She told me she was still in academia, this time at Victoria University. She found tutoring really hard and preferred just to do research by herself. She then apologised for going on about herself for too long. I assured her I didn't mind in the least.

I started talking about myself – something I hate doing – then we fell into a mutual round of apologising for going on about ourselves too much. The interaction ended with her apologising because she had to leave to catch her bus. As we parted ways, she gave me a hug and apologised for getting her hair stuck in my stubble. As she walked off, I saw her apologising to some oblivious man who had walked straight into her. There's no other way to describe this woman, at this point, than as a very sorry sight.

THE OFFICIOUS NEW ZEALANDER

The Officious New Zealander is a pedantic rule-follower, even when following the rules negates all common sense or, more irritatingly, when it is no skin off their nose if the rules are broken.

I'm reminded of a man at one of the first gyms I went to. There was a sign above the exercycles that said, 'Please limit the usage of these bikes to 20 minutes.'

He and I were the only ones in the gym this day, and he was on a rowing machine while I was on one of the six exercycles.

After 20 minutes on the bike, I went into the five-minute cool-down period and my new mate sauntered around and looked over my shoulder. Then he leaned in.

'Ah, read the sign, mate.'

'What?'

'It's a maximum of twenty minutes per machine.'

I frowned at him but kept cycling.

'Oi, mate! It's a twenty-minute maximum. You've done more than twenty minutes. Would you like me to go and tell the head trainer?'

I shook my head.

He must've been twice my age and I was afraid of authority, so I got off the bike. He just shook his head at me and sauntered off.

I was suddenly so filled with rage that I promptly got onto the bike beside the one I'd just been on. I thought this was a great 'fuck you' but he didn't even see. And I had to keep cycling even though I was exhausted, both so I could save face and in the hope that he would see me.

Later, I was temping at yet another office in South Auckland. It was in an industrial zone, so there were lots of carparks for transport trucks and big warehouses, and this high-tech office where I worked.

I was working reception with another temp, who was Australian. We ended up having a great laugh together and we both knew how to play the game of temping. Every other day, one of us would take an extended lunchtime and get covered by the other.

Also in the office was this little Officious New Zealander walking around in his nylon office pants. Let's call him Brett. He was short and slight and had skin that I can't imagine had ever seen much sun. He worked in the accounting department but took it upon himself to police the whole office (even though it wasn't his job).

I first bore the brunt of Brett when I came back after an hour-and-fifteen-minute lunch break. He walked out of his office, head held high and eyebrows raised even higher, and tapped his little fist onto the plexiglass reception desk as he passed us, then – without breaking his stride – said, 'You left at one o'clock. It's now two fifteen.' He then continued around the corner and out of sight.

I flushed bright red and looked to my co-receptionist.

'Was that the big boss?' I asked.

'I don't think so. I think he just works in the accounting department.'

I spent the rest of the day waiting to get fired, but it never happened. My manager and the two levels of bosses higher up were very pleasant when they saw me.

The next day, I was making a coffee whilst the co-receptionist was out for lunch. Lil' Brett thrust his head into the staffroom with the same raised eyebrows he'd used on me the previous day.

'Why on earth is there no one at reception? Someone is waiting there,' he said, then left, barely breaking his stride.

I ran around to the reception desk to find a courier waiting patiently and not at all miffed that the desk was unmanned.

The next day, we managed to squirrel away a couple of pastries that had been destined for a meeting and we planned to eat them whilst hidden behind our desk.

Brett strode past and did his favourite rat-a-tat-tat with his fist on the plexiglass, before telling us that the pastries in the staffroom were for the marketing staff. Somehow, he'd found out we'd nicked some and was reprimanding us for it – and we thought we had been so careful!

The next week, he handed me a sheet of printed paper. It was my CV. I'd been working on it during my shift and had printed it out. Why, dear God, did *he* have to be the one to pick it up?

'Just a reminder,' he told me, 'the printer's not for private printing.'

I apologised profusely whilst wondering why he cared. If I were in his position, I wouldn't have given a shit what anyone else did.

A few days later, there was a rat-a-tat-tat on the desk and I was told that I was five minutes late for my shift. By this point, I was no longer embarrassed or guilty. I just hated him. My co-receptionist hated him more, thankfully, and when she came back from lunch, literally on the hour, he came over, with his eyebrows high, to inform her she was late.

'I'm actually on time,' she said.

Brett was taken aback that someone was standing up to him. But he was ready with a comeback.

'You walked through the door on the hour, but you went to put your bag and coat away. The hour's lunch is from leaving the desk to returning to the desk.'

'Are you in charge of the receptionists?' she asked, showing far more chutzpah than I ever could.

He hesitated. 'No.'

'Oh, sorry. I just assumed you must've been.'

'I'm in the accounting department.'

'Oh ...' She played confused very well. 'Oh, okay. I just assumed you'd only worry about my lunch break if you were in charge of reception.'

Brett's eyes narrowed slightly. 'Anyway,' he said, 'I suggest you be back at your desk within the hour, otherwise you'll piss Simon off.' Simon was the boss.

'Okay, cool, because I wasn't told that was the rule.'

'Well, it is,' Brett said.

'Okay,' said my co-receptionist, her feigned nonchalance boiling his blood.

They stared at each other. It was a stand-off. He then headed straight for Simon's office. We both watched as he rat-a-tat-tatted on the door and was invited in.

The blinds on the glass wall were half-closed but we could see Brett talking to Simon. He stayed in there for less than two minutes then walked back to his desk whilst avoiding eye contact with us. He never reprimanded us ever again. I have no idea what Simon had told Brett, but I hope it was something along the lines of, 'Just chill the fuck out.'

THE ARTS ADMINISTRATOR

The ladies we are about to discuss are the lifeblood of art and culture in Aotearoa. They are 'of a certain age' – let's say 45 to 65 – and I like to call them the Arts Administrators. Yes, there are younger women who work in arts administration (and they will definitely evolve into *this* particular breed of women), but in order to fully become the magnificence of an Arts Administrator, you need to have lived a bit, seen a lot, developed an artistic aesthetic – but never been artistic yourself.

Occasionally these women come from artistic backgrounds, but I find that particular subspecies have a deep bitterness within them. They treat artists with thinly veiled disdain.

On the other hand, the best of the Arts Administrators are open about having no artistic skills themselves. They simply want to facilitate the best outcomes for the artists they're dealing with. And, boy, if they manage to launch the career of an artist then they will die very happy women.

The Arts Administrator can be found in galleries, theatres, festivals and, at a pinch, community centres throughout the country. They come in all shapes and sizes – tall and very slender to basically a round ball. However, there are three defining characteristics of the Arts Administrator. Number one is the statement hairstyle. Again, these hairstyles come in a wide variety, but they are all considered and definitely make an impression. There's the shockingly bright white pixie cut, the orange bob with severe fringe and the waist-length jet-black hair wound into a bun, to name but a few.

Their outfits may vary from a range of shades of black, and only black, to bright and colourful flower-prints, but they always have statement frames for their glasses. Severe black block frames are always a go-to for these women.

Their third defining aesthetic choice is a pounamu resting upon their chests, or a chunky pounamu ring on their finger, or maybe some delicate silver kowhai flower earrings – just something 'cultural'.

These women also love to discuss kaupapa. They're always talking about the kaupapa of the institution they work for. They're always middle-aged white women but their use of te reo really puts the rest of us to shame.

One such Arts Administrator I met ran a gallery in Whanganui where I was attending a wedding. She was wearing severe black-framed glasses, a chiffon sack dress, black stockings and black heels. She had a wayward mass of greying hair with some loose strands, but the bulk of her hair was held together with a thin pounamu pin.

As the wedding guests arrived, she walked around neurotically, making sure none of the gallery's artworks were being touched. Intrigued by this character, I went up, introduced myself and complimented her on her choice of the artists she was exhibiting.

She promptly rattled off a list of all the artists she had ever exhibited. She seemed to believe that I knew who they all were. Unfortunately, I did not recognise a single name, but I nodded appreciatively anyway.

I've spent some time analysing and enjoying another quintessential Arts Administrator from afar. This one ran a major city arts festival. She had long, grey hair twirled up into a bun at an age when most women go short. She loved the colour orange and even sported an orange lipstick from time to time. She was considered by all to be a stalwart of New Zealand culture and was responsible for bringing over the most peculiar international artists to impose themselves upon the tiny percentage of New Zealanders who attend art events.

She just loved the responsibility that came with educating the populace on what real 'culture' was. If you were an artist and were completely misunderstood and ostracised by the rest of New Zealand, she would be right there by your side. 'You're too advanced for them,' she'd say. 'You're well before your time, you'd do much better in Europe. They understand true art over there.'

Another Arts Administrator I met was the facilitator of a festival in one of New Zealand's smaller cities. She had blackberry hair and severe, black-framed glasses. I was in the city for three nights and each night she wore a different coloured pashmina slung around her shoulders with her pounamu hanging over the top of it. The opening night of the festival was sponsored by a local house-painting company.

The festival included a solo show by a brooding young dancer. When I attend these things the artwork's meaning often goes completely over my head. I'm never sure what the artist is trying to communicate, and it all feels, dare I say it, a bit pretentious. Usually, the rest of the audience seem to be in awe, however, gasping quietly and shaking their heads in disbelief at the utter transcendent brilliance happening on the stage in front of them. This night was different.

The audience seemed disengaged, then the shifting in the seats started, then the sighing, and then there was the obligatory old man falling asleep in the front row. When the recital ended, there was no standing ovation nor cheering for a second bow. The dancer didn't seem to mind, however. If he'd even noticed the reaction, he probably just thought everyone in the audience was beneath him.

Afterwards, our Arts Administrator heroine took to the lectern in the foyer and enthusiastically thanked all the sponsors and talked about what an amazing show it had been. She then invited the dancer up onto the stage. He didn't have much of a speech prepared but thanked a few people, yet forgot to mention the Arts Administrator heroine beside him. I watched her as he shuffled off the tiny stage. Her smile was plastered to her face, but her eyes couldn't hide her hurt.

Later, amidst the hustle and bustle of platters of salmon, cream cheese and capers on tiny pancakes being passed around, I sidled close to our heroine. She was being congratulated by everyone. At one point, however, she was alone with someone who seemed to be a trusted friend.

She grabbed the friend by the wrist and leant in. In a whisper, she asked, 'Was it absolutely terrible?'

Her friend hesitated before answering, 'No, it was great,' as convincingly as she could.

'Oh good, because he's such an up-and-comer and I wanted to give him this opportunity. I can just see him taking on the world.'

SECURITY GUARDS

There are certain people in the world who don't make much of an impact on their surroundings. They just kind of disappear into the scenery and, if you ask anyone, no one will remember that these people were even there. That's what I feel Security Guards are like. They're just kinda there. I know they should probably exude an air of authority, creating an underlying fear in everyone so no one breaks the rules, but I haven't come across many who actually achieve this.

I also wonder how observant Security Guards need to be. Is it just their presence that is required? What is going on in their brains? Are they watching everything like a hawk? Or, to survive all the long hours, do they need to go into a zen-like state?

There was this one time when a clothing store's huge storefront window had been smashed. A young Security Guard was standing beside the gaping hole in the window. For a while, I didn't notice him. I'd even spent some time examining the hole before I realised someone was standing beside me.

'Oh, hello,' I said, feeling particularly nosey.

He nodded and smiled.

We stood there in silence, not far from each other, and I decided that wouldn't do. I'd need to interact with this guy.

'What happened?' I asked.

He hesitated for a moment, then the words flowed forth. It was almost like he had been desperate to talk to someone. He explained how two thieves had smashed the glass and slipped in through the hole, cutting themselves and dripping blood everywhere as they went.

They then had the opportunity to steal tens of thousands of dollars' worth of handbags, because the store sold very expensive handbags, which were all right there for the taking. But they chose not to. They only stole $800 worth of bags.

Both the Security Guard and I mused on how that was very strange. We then tried to work out what the psychology had been behind not taking more stuff. He told me that burglars often come back to the places they had previously been, so we tried to work out the psychology behind that as well.

With that conversation topic expended, I asked the Security Guard how he passed his day. He was very frank with me. He told me that every 15 minutes he would walk around the perimeter of the premises, which took about three minutes, and the rest of the time stood by the broken window. The only thing he did other than that was checking his phone for messages. He was trying to sell his car at the time, and he was also chatting to a girl online.

I was very pleased by his honesty but then the conversation seemed to sour. He asked me why I wanted to know. I told him I was just interested. He nodded and folded his arms. It wasn't until the next morning, as I was brushing my teeth, that I realised he might've thought I was one of the burglars returning to the place I had previously robbed!

I once had a job selling floral aquariums and retractable hoses in the central thoroughfare of a mall. Trying to get passers-by interested in these shoddily made piles of crap was absolute agony. The one highlight was my burgeoning friendship with a Security Guard. We'll call him Kalepo.

It took a few days to notice him as he casually strolled up the promenade, then waited a few minutes outside Living and Giving, before turning back and strolling to Paper Plus, hovering outside there for a few moments and then repeating the circuit. When I finally noticed him, he was always ready with a smile and a pump of the eyebrows.

I was too shy to go up to people to sell the floral aquariums, so I would hover behind the counter, wishing my life was over, but also desperately in need of the minimum wage I was earning. When the bosses were around, I would force myself to approach people who clearly didn't want to be approached. When the bosses weren't around, I sat back and read my book, hiding it from view beneath the counter.

One time, I was nearly caught reading by my boss, who we'll call Wayne. I happened to look up seconds before he descended upon the booth. I chucked the book in amongst the retractable hoses and cultivated my face into one of a go-getter. I guess Kalepo must've seen this happen because from then on, whenever he noticed Wayne approaching, he'd do a quick whistle. I'd look over, he'd pump his eyebrows and I knew what was up. I'd hide my book with plenty of time then venture out into the weak stream of potential customers and hock my wares. I really appreciated Kalepo for that.

Kalepo's stint in that mall was short lived, however. I was in there with him over the silly season, when there were literally only six Christmas carols playing on repeat: 'Jingle Bells', 'Jingle Bell Rock', 'Frosty the Snowman', 'We Wish You A Merry Christmas', 'Deck the Halls' and 'Feliz Navidad'.

I quickly developed the ability to zone the carols out, but they seemed to irritate Kalepo. As the days passed, his energy became increasingly agitated. When 'Feliz Navidad' would play – yet again – he would let out an audible sigh. I'd look over and he'd be mouthing along to the words, but his facial expressions suggested he didn't want to be doing that. At one point, 'Frosty the Snowman' started again, and he dragged his finger over his eyes and down over his cheeks, pulling his flesh downwards before shaking his head and pressing the palms of his hands into his eye sockets.

As the days progressed, his complexion became decidedly grey, and – despite his best efforts – his fingers thrummed against his thighs in time to 'Jingle Bells'. Then he just disappeared.

I arrived one day at work and he was gone. The next day I asked his replacement where Kalepo had gone and was told he'd asked for a transfer to a carpark out east – one without any Christmas carols, hopefully.

I did miss him, though … and the lack of his warning whistle led to my eventual downfall. I got caught in the act of reading and was promptly fired.

THE JACK OF ALL TRADES

I've worked on foreign film sets. Doing, like, the lowest of the lowest jobs. Like, basically, my job was making sure the Tupperware container of nuts/cranberry mix was always full and people had water.

The thing you notice on these foreign film sets is that people have their specific jobs and they stick to them. They never help with anyone else's tasks. For example, say the sound guy is standing beside a heavy light on a tall stand and it's about to fall. Instead of steadying it, he'll just stand there and watch it tip over because it's not his department.

On Kiwi film sets, on the other hand, there's a sense of everyone mucking in and helping each other. Not only the sound guy, but also the make-up artist, someone from the art department and a couple of actors would all run over to make sure that tipping heavy light was set back on its feet. It's because we are a nation of Jacks of All Trades. I think the small population and our relatively egalitarian society mean we all do whatever it takes to get by.

In my time, I've met a few Kiwis who have the ability to step into any job, no matter how disparate, and make a real success of it. But no one can rival one woman I'm going to call Kate.

One night she'd been at a restaurant as a paying customer when she heard that the chef had had a motorcycle accident. She offered to step into the role. Let me clarify that situation. She was there for dinner with friends and the chef didn't show up, so Kate abandoned her friends, walked through the saloon doors into the kitchen and simply took over.

I met Kate at one of my first jobs. I spent one summer waiting tables and she was in charge of the kitchen. And, boy, she was good at it. She always had a smile on her face. When I found out about how she'd got the job, I asked her if she had run a kitchen before.

'God, no,' she said, then told me she had waited tables on a cruise liner once and had also been a cook's assistant on an oil rig, so she knew the gist of it.

Running a kitchen must be one of the most stressful jobs ever, but Kate kept it fun. She would always find five minutes to have a cigarette break and down a shandy before getting back to work.

'Okay, how do we do this?' she'd ask, as she put on her glasses and glanced over a recipe for coq au vin. She'd scan her finger over the instructions then screw up her face. 'Let's just wing it, shall we?'

Then she'd somehow create a coq au vin about which the customer would ask the waiter to pass on their compliments to the chef.

Kate moved on from the restaurant not long after I left, but over the coming years, whenever I returned home I would run into her working at the petrol station, painting houses, cleaning motels, managing hotels, working at a garden centre, picking fruit, working as a doctor's receptionist and then stepping up as a nurse without any qualifications.

She loved travelling around the country and would head off on adventures with a deep sense that everything would work out for her. Once she was travelling south by train and just mucked in in the train's kitchen, serving everyone their sandwiches in triangular plastic containers. She ended up doing that for a few weeks before getting a job at a vineyard selling wine to tourists.

Kate had a wonderful knack for getting on with everyone and loved to do the sly wink at you when she was pulling someone else's leg – and she was always pulling someone's leg. She was a real larrikin.

Another thing she loved was making connections between people. 'Oh, you're from Alexandra, are ya? What's your last name? Thompson? You wouldn't happen to be any relation of Ian Thompson from Alex, would ya? He's ya uncle? I used to kick around with him when we were plucking turkeys up in Whangarei. How is the old bastard? Is he? I bet he is. He could put away a few Lion Reds if I remember rightly.'

I didn't know much about her romantic life, but she was jovially flirtatious with every man she met. They always seemed to know she was up for a bit of teasing and gentle ribbing.

Despite not having a family of her own, she was always around when one of her girlfriend's gave birth, providing whatever support she could. She then became an aunty figure for all of the resulting children. If the newborn child's father needed to spend more time with the baby, she'd just step into his accounting firm and run the place successfully until he was ready to return.

I kinda forgot about Kate for years until I was over in Melbourne one time. I was innocently walking through Fitzroy with a friend when who should walk down the street but bloody Kate!

'How are ya, ya bastard?' she asked as she winked at my companion.

'What are you doing over here, Kate?'

'I was travelling through the outback and somehow found myself working with some Aboriginals in their health centre, so I've been doing that for the last six months. Before that I was sleeping my way across Australia working in sheepo.' (A sheepo helps shearing teams get the sheep through the shearing process.)

'Sleeping your way through?'

'Yeah,' she said and winked at me. 'But, my god, working with the Aboriginals can be a laugh. They've got a great sense of humour. They're always telling me they're paining.'

'Painting?'

'No. Paining, as in they're in pain. But it's only so they can get their hands on the painkillers and get out of it.' Her face became serious. 'There's some deep trauma they need to work through, I reckon. Anyway, I'll stick with it until I've gotta get up to Darwin.'

'What are you doing up there?'

'My girlfriend's insisting I come up and work at the new resort they've opened up there.'

'What will you be doing?'

'Whatever needs to be done, mate,' she said as she gave me one of her good old winks.

THE UNDERAPPRECIATED UNDERLING

There is a specific kind of New Zealander I call the Underappreciated Underling. They are invariably on the lower rungs within a workplace hierarchy and their bitterness about that fact is palpable. Resentment for those in higher positions is prevalent. Unfortunately, those further up the hierarchy are usually completely oblivious to the Underappreciated Underling's anguish – either that or they just don't care.

I once did a gig for a leading Australasian bank. The organisers wanted a humorous interlude in the middle of a seminar in an event centre in downtown Auckland at which all of their employees from around the country had congregated.

My friend and I decided to do a bogus motivational speech. We thought we'd take the piss out of motivational slogans and business speak, so we wrote a piece that went something like: 'Let's hit the ground running with a game-changer action plan that will value-add to organic growth whilst keeping the moving parts thinking outside the box.'

My friend and I thought it was hilarious. We wrote the script and had ourselves in hysterics. Little did we know that we were setting ourselves up for the worst night of our lives.

Now, these kinds of things are usually organised by the 'social events' coordinator for the organisation. Think a perky young woman, who is very savvy with social media and pop culture. The one we were dealing with for this particular event was a huge fan of ours and kept assuring us that we were going to be so great.

The problem was these kinds of people don't tend to be indicative of the company at large. And at a bank? I would say the majority were very strait-laced, sensible sort of people over whose heads our piss-taking, kooky sort of comedy would go. But anyway ...

We arrived at the venue an hour before showtime. The venue staff were walking around in their formal shirts and black trousers, the women with their hair up in buns, and the men with copious gel slicking back their manes. We headed straight to three skinny men seated in the back of a carpeted room. They were wearing all black. This was the tech crew, seated behind their sound and lighting desks with those black box things with all the knobs. You know the type I'm talking about? Wires everywhere.

We focused on the eldest man amongst them. He would have been in his mid-forties. The two others would have been in their late teens/early twenties. Our hero was bald with salt'n'pepper hair around the fringes and a salt'n'pepper goatee. He was leaning back in his chair, throwing a small ball up and down and having a laugh with the other two.

We introduced ourselves and I saw a flash of annoyance that they had to do some work now. We explained what we wanted to do. We had this slideshow on our laptop and we wanted to connect it to the big screen somehow, so I could work the laptop and slideshow while I was on stage.

He shook his head. 'We haven't got the ability to do that,' he said, flatly.

My friend and I tensed. Our entire presentation relied on the slideshow of mountain scenes with terrible motivational quotes written over them.

He shrugged. 'If you'd given me a bit of warning, I might have been able to organise something for you. But, I'm sorry, you'll have to come up with something else.'

His tone was very … not dismissive exactly, more one of annoyance. He was annoyed at us. It was as if we were being rude to him.

My friend and I stepped aside to discuss the situation. What the hell were we going to do? Could we just describe what was on the slideshow to the audience? That wouldn't work! What else could we do? What else could we do? What else could we do?

We turned back to the tech guy and pleaded. 'Is there any way we could possibly make this work?'

We told him we'd explained our idea to the social events coordinator for the bank and she had said it was great. Never once did she mention that doing a slideshow would be a problem.

He shrugged. 'Like I said, if you'd given me some warning, I would have been able to organise the right cables for you.'

Thankfully, just at that point, we saw the social events coordinator walk into the room. We waved her over and explained the situation. She was clearly of higher rank than this Underappreciated Underling. She asked him if there was someone he could ask to help, as there simply had to be a solution.

The Underappreciated Underling glared at her, then shrugged. He said he'd ask around but he couldn't make any promises. He then muttered something as he walked off.

The social events coordinator smiled at us, completely oblivious to his resentment, then assured us we were going to be beloved by all the bankers that night. Our hero found the necessary cable within two minutes.

He then took his sweet time, setting the cable up and connecting it to our laptop. I watched him as he crawled around the tables. By the time he reached the stage, where I was standing, I'd worked out how to play his game.

'Thank you so much,' I said a little too effusively.

He shrugged and avoided eye contact. 'Like I said, if you'd given me some warning, we wouldn't be in this situation.'

I nodded.

'Give us your computer,' he said with a pissed-off sigh.

I handed it over and launched my next counter-attack. 'Honestly,' I said, 'I don't know how you do it. I wouldn't know the first thing about cables.'

He shrugged, then gave a thumbs-up to one of the 19-year-olds at the desk.

'And all those knobs on your desk – how long did it take you to learn how to do all that?'

'Oh …' He thought for a moment. 'I started thirty years ago, but, I mean, technology has changed.'

'Absolutely. And do you have to retrain to know how to work it?'

'Nah, I learn on the job.'

'Wow! I just … I honestly don't know how you guys do it.'

Suddenly the first slide of the slideshow appeared on the screen behind me. Disaster averted.

'Oh, thank you so much,' I said, beaming love at him.

'No problem.' He shrugged, even though it was clear he needed this appreciation. 'And, like I said, next time give me a bit of warning and we can avoid all of that.'

'Honestly,' I told him, 'you are an absolute lifesaver.'

And, just like that, I had won him over. All he needed was a little bit of appreciation and suddenly he was all over us, making sure we had enough water, making jokes about bankers, giving us a wink when it was 'showtime'.

None of that combated the travesty that was our presentation. We completely bombed. None of the jokes landed, and we looked out at a sea of unimpressed faces. We dropped the last part of our performance then scurried backstage where we sat in the green room, completely despondent, compulsively eating from our complimentary platter.

Just then, the Underappreciated Underling walked in to take off our head mics.

'That was tough,' I said.

'Don't worry about them,' he told us. 'These bankers are a bunch of wankers that wouldn't know what funny was if it bit them in the ass.'

Bless that embittered, sad, sad, goatee-wearing man.

THE UNEMPLOYABLES

Life is tough for the unemployed. I was on the dole for six weeks once and I hated it. I was forever having to prove I was looking for work, being made to feel like absolute shit for shuffling into WINZ, then sitting around with all the other dishevelled, downcast lot as I was taken through the obligatory seminar and then told I couldn't claim the dole because my partner made the minimum wage. The ones that manage to cheat the system? I feel they should be given trophies for their canniness and their ability to live off such little money.

I've met a few people on the dole in my time, as there are many artists who just have to claim it. My favourite wasn't an artist, though. He was a total treasure who we'll call Terry. He was the flatmate of someone I dated for six months. The flat hadn't been touched since the 1950s. It was 10 minutes from downtown Auckland but was nestled in bush. It was on a wee isthmus and the owners had chosen to do nothing with the land, nor the house.

Terry was always at home and he was often drunk. Beers were his drink of choice. He was one of those people who explain things too much.

'If you just move the car, I'll be able to get the recycling bin out.'

'No worries.'

I moved my car.

'Thanks, mate. I just needed you to do that so I could get the recycling bin out.'

'Of course.'

'You can usually park there, no worries. Just when the recycling needs to be taken out, I'll need to get access to it.'

'Of course.'

'Even if you had parked a metre further away from the garage, I would have been able to get the recycling bin out.'

'Yip.'

'But the way you had parked, I just wouldn't have been able to manage it.'

'Cool.'

And so on, and so on.

He was terribly lonely and would use any opportunity to knock on the door and begin a conversation.

'Hey, sorry to disturb, I'm just about to put the recycling out. Is there anything you want to add?'

'Nah, we're okay.'

'Okay. Hey, did you watch the game last night?'

His nemesis for a stage was a tui that had made its home in a nearby banksia tree. I've got to admit, the few times I was there, the tui was very annoying. But, I guess, being at home all the time, Terry had been pushed over the edge by it, so he decided to take matters into his own hands. He got his hands on a shotgun and eventually killed the tui. Such crimes, apparently, come with a $100,000 fine, but no one ever dobbed him in.

He was always claiming he was in the process of getting work, and it was always in ambitious careers. Keeping in mind he hadn't worked for 10 years, he claimed he was in talks to work for big-time recruitment companies.

He would occasionally leave in the afternoon to go and meet with these various companies. He would dress up in a shirt and tie that always looked a little unkempt, but nothing could disguise his alcoholic ruddiness.

Later, he'd come back, with a takeaway Domino's pizza, claiming the meeting had gone really well. But he never seemed to get the job.

He did, however, have a scheme to make some extra cash on the side. There was some prime billboard real estate beside a road passing through the isthmus. Someone must've asked him if they could use it and he said yes. He got paid thousands of dollars for the advertising on it. Technically the money should have gone to the landowners, but it took them a couple of years to catch on to what was going on. They asked Terry if he knew anything about it, but he feigned ignorance. He didn't know who the advertising company was, or why they'd decided to use the billboard space. He then promptly disappeared. Like, moved out of the city never to be seen again.

Last I heard, he'd floated down to his parents' place in the Coromandel somewhere, so he was probably telling them about all the potential recruitment jobs that were coming his way.

I met another Unemployable treasure when I was working at the Matamata franchise of a large international fried chicken company one summer. We'll call him Mitchell.

It was a horrible job. My manager used to mock my voice, and I had to wear a women's pink fitted uniform because they were out of men's ones. Every week I would explain that I couldn't work the Friday night or the Sunday shift because that was when I stacked shelves at New World. I would then promptly be rostered on for those exact shifts. I would then be told that it was my responsibility to get them covered by someone else within the team.

Mitchell worked in the kitchen and I worked the till. Mitchell was one of the few co-workers who was nice to me. He was always making jokes and would take time out of his day to explain how to do the various tasks, especially how to scoop the mass-produced mashed potato into the gravy. He always had bloodshot eyes and was always diligent about taking his breaks. He told me later that he had been on the dole for six years before landing the job, so he was super excited about getting it. And he worked hard to keep it.

Anyway, one Saturday I showed up for work at 10 am. It was just me, another girl (wearing the same pink uniform as me) working the till and Mitchell, who was working the kitchen. The girl behind the till had had a huge night on the piss and had eyes bloodshot to buggery. At one point, she began an order with a customer then signalled to me to finish up the purchase as she stepped into the office area to control some dry retching.

Half an hour later, thankfully with no customers in the store, she proceeded to throw up. I distinctly remember half-eaten mushroom scattered across the brown concrete floor. This made Mitchell throw up as well. He wasn't hungover, or sick, but the mere sight of someone else throwing up instantly tipped him over the edge. There was vomit everywhere.

I quickly fetched the industrial-strength hose, which they used to clean the premises every night, and I hosed the evidence down the grated gutter in the corner of the kitchen. The whole thing was disgusting.

The following Monday, we were all called into work and both the vomiters were fired. I feebly tried to argue on Mitchell's behalf, explaining his vomiting had been sympathy motivated, but it did him no good. As he was packing up his locker, I offered him my condolences. He shrugged and simply said: 'This is always how it goes.'

Six months passed before I saw Mitchell again. He was in town, a little worse for wear with fuzzy hair going every which way, stubble and wearing a ratty Swanndri. I asked him what he was up to these days. He shrugged. He was on the dole again but had recently been in hospital because one of the couches he'd lit on fire had gone a bit AWOL. He showed me his bandaged leg. I decided not to ask him the specifics of why he'd been burning a couch.

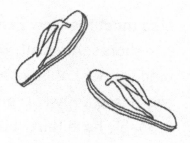

KIWIS OUTDOORS AND OVERSEAS

Aotearoa is a major tourist destination and with good reason. We have so many beautiful views and outdoor activities in which to partake. If I had a dollar for every time someone said, 'In New Zealand, you can ski the mountains in the morning then be surfing at the beach that afternoon,' I'd have four dollars.

There is a lot of wilderness here and grand national parks and a huge amount of coastline. Populating these areas are some fairly interesting human case studies, so let's meet the New Zealanders of the coast and the bush. And let us also meet the New Zealanders who have left our fair shores. After all, we're a nation of journeymen (and women). If I had a dollar for every time I'd overheard a Kiwi accent in a foreign locale, I'd probably have thirty bucks.

BOATIES

I have just this very afternoon attended a boat show. There I discovered a very specific breed of New Zealand man. Let's call them Boaties.

As I walked past the various stalls, I swear I saw the same man three times but, no, they were just cookie-cutter versions of the same model.

Let me paint the picture. Every one of these men had a ruddiness to his complexion. This is, no doubt, from being out in the scorching sun whenever he gets the chance. Their lips and the tops of their ears were invariably chapped. Their hair, if not grey, was at least salt'n'pepper, and receding. Their necks were red with stray white hairs sprouting from them. Their hands were meaty, no doubt from gripping that boat wheel hard, or from forever dealing with ropes. They all wore gold wedding rings on their swollen red fingers, each of which ended with a considerable fingernail. They all wore sunglasses either over their eyes or on top of their heads. The sunglasses were always of the streamlined variety – a wraparound, as it's known in the biz. The arms of their glasses were tucked into a strip of wetsuit material so that, if they fell off, they would sit around the Boatie's neck instead of falling into the ocean.

These men all wore polo shirts, usually white, sometimes black. Never any other colour. The shirt was never tucked in and would hang over the distended bellies of the portlier of the species. They also all wore black trousers. And their legs would end in, perhaps not surprisingly, boat shoes. I presumed this was a uniform for the men working in the stalls. But no, it was worn both by those working there and the common punter who'd come to have a mosey around. They would all stand with their legs apart, creating a very firm, steady pose. Their meaty hands would be resting on their hips, the skin whitening (or yellowing) around the creases and knuckles.

Every corner I turned at that boat show had another pair of men chewing the fat as they leaned against a motor, or a battery, or a mock-up of the 'never slip' faux-wood stair covers with sandpaper-like grip panels. I leaned in close to one conversation ...

'Yeah, John actually ended up selling that catamaran.'

'Is that right?'

'And bought himself a Hartley thirty-footer.'

'Is that right?'

'Yeah.'

Silence falls for a moment.

'How's that working out for him?'

'What's that?'

'The Hartley?'

'Yeah, once he changed the motor it went like a dream.'

I walked into a life-jacket stall showing a variety of life-jackets I had never thought possible. There I overheard a second conversation ...

'Guess how much the Aquila went for.'

'Oh god. Ah, a hundred k?'

'Try five hundred k.'

'Shit. Is that right? And he forked that out?'

'Yeah.'

'Rich bastards.'

'He's taking it around the islands.'

'Is that right?'

'Eventually wants to take it around the world before his eyesight goes.'

'Is that right?'

I ventured outside and, after flashing my wristband, was allowed onto the marina where I could walk onto the luxury launches. More of these men were walking around with slim wives.

'What did you think about that?' one of the men asked his wife as they stepped off an 18-foot launch that glistened in all its extravagant whiteness.

'I don't know about the price tag,' she muttered under her breath.

At this, her husband's face drooped and the sparkle left his eyes.

I approached the largest boat in the line-up. Three men stood on the back deck. They were in a uniform of black polo shirts and white trousers.

I removed my boots and was given a tour of the boat. It was a luxury liner as far as I could tell. The man taking me on the tour spoke with great glee about how long the boat was, how many knots it could do and the fact that it had a salt-water conversion system for the onboard shower.

I asked if *he* wanted a boat like this and he said he preferred fishing boats.

This particular boat belonged to a Swiss billionaire. The man showing me around told me he'd tried to find out how the billionaire had made his money but, 'as with most of our rich clients, they like to keep under the radar. We couldn't find anything on him.'

I looked over the extreme decadence of the boat, appreciating the bowl of fresh fruit on the fastened-down table. I later found similar bowls on all the other launches. I'm not sure what they were trying to achieve with these props. Maybe it was a subtle message to take precautions around scurvy when you're on the high seas ...

I continued around the marina, passing more men in white or black polo shirts until I came to the fishing boat tent. There I discovered a subspecies of Boaties. These ones were still wearing polo shirts, but they were wearing shorts instead of trousers, and these shorts ended just below the knee. They also wore wraparound sunglasses but these men all had caps on too.

There were stalls advertising fishing lines and in each one a man showed another similar-looking man the best way to cast a specific rod. At another stall, an enthusiastic man seemed to be re-enacting a fish thrashing through the water.

Two similar-looking men watched on with their hands on their hips and the creases of their fingers whitening.

I moseyed up to another stall and hovered near another conversation ...

'Yeah, he got himself twelve snapper within minutes he said.'

'Is that right?'

'Went back there the next day and got nothing.'

'Is that right?'

'Yeah.'

Silence fell for a moment. The original man cleared his throat then resumed speaking.

'Yeah, I went to check it out and only got little fuckers. Had to chuck 'em all back.'

'Shame.'

'Yeah.'

Silence fell again.

'Anyway, mate, it was good to see ya.'

'Yeah, you too. Catch ya round, eh?'

Then they shook hands and carried on their merry ways.

THE ALPHA MALE TEENAGER

You notice these fellows at various beachside and lakeside towns in the build-up to and aftermath of New Year's Eve. Of course, they are around throughout the year, but this is the time when you'll notice them the most. They are the Alpha Male Teenager.

Alpha Male Teenagers exist in packs. They spend the majority of their time trying to impress each other. This can involve doing pranks or daredevil stunts, drinking copious amounts of alcohol, having prowess with the opposite sex, loudly driving around in their cars and just being a boisterous energy in public.

This type of Kiwi loves jumping off high things into water. If there's a pool beside a house, they'll climb onto the roof and jump off. After which they will either land in the water or destroy their bodies by falling onto the concrete.

This is the type of Kiwi who will vomit beer into a yard glass then drink it again. This is the type of Kiwi who whips his mates with a towel in the changing rooms. This is also the type of Kiwi whose mothers will do anything for them. When they are older, they will be visited by their mothers, who will do their laundry for them at their flats. This is because the Alpha Male Teenager is incapable of basic self-care.

Alpha Male Teenagers wear caps, singlets and board shorts. If they wear anything on their feet, it will be jandals, otherwise they just have bare, tanned, broad feet with huge toenails. Their leg hairs glisten gold because of all the bleaching sun they have been getting.

They have a general vibe of sportiness. Some of them surf. A lot of them play rugby. There is sometimes a portly individual amongst the group (usually a prop in the rugby team) who is often the butt of jokes but who, when he finally 'scores' a chick, is fondly congratulated by the others.

I have been privy to the Alpha Male Teenager both by being at their parties and also through being harassed by them. The latter involved me attempting to begin a new year with the attitude of 'New Year, New Me'.

I was doing a sweaty/cumbersome jog along the beach of Mount Maunganui on the morning of 1 January when I made the mistake of running past a pack of Alpha Male Teenagers. One of them ran along beside me for 30 or so metres, much to the enjoyment of his peers. I smiled along, like an idiot, wishing the humiliation would just be over. The night before, however, the Alpha Male Teenagers would have been completely oblivious to my presence.

For them, celebrations begin early on New Year's Eve – say, around midday. A collection of white, plastic, fan-backed chairs are placed in a ring, then various boxes of beers are torn open and divvied out.

They sit around, throwing a ball sometimes, or waxing lyrical about strangely philosophical matters, and then the female contingent show up. These girls have long hair, short dresses and are always in pairs. These girls feign feebleness and allow their male counterparts to appear infinitely more physical, more capable and more clever than they are. The boys will skateboard around, showing off their skills, and the girls will demand a try on the board then cock up, scream, fall over and laugh uproariously.

As the night approaches, they all head down to the beach where they form bigger mobs. There are messengers, mostly girls, sharing information from one mob to another. The universally-decided-upon hottest Alpha Male and equivalent Alpha Female pair off. They move further along the beach. He'll still be in his singlet. She'll have a large jumper on with the sleeve ends gripped tightly in her hands, as if she's cold, but her smooth legs will be bare. Some kissing will, no doubt, take place. And maybe even more.

The thing about the Alpha Male Teenager is that New Zealand society has been designed for them. They appear to get everything they could possibly want. They start off with good genes because their parents were no doubt the Alphas of their generation. They are sporty, and sports is the pinnacle of New Zealand life. They can be naughty but are always forgiven. They leave school and appear to fall into exactly the career path they want, usually with the help of some nepotism along the way.

Because they don't know what real struggle is, you can rest assured they evolve into the dullest adults possible. And, with any luck, they'll be hit by early hair loss, whilst piling on the kilos and ruing the fact they never pushed themselves with their rugby as they could have been an All Black.

In my final year at school I had been lucky (unlucky) enough to spend New Year's Eve at a party with an Alpha Male Teenager. He had sat around in the ring of white, plastic, fan-backed chairs and philosophically queried why the male testicle didn't evolve a pain-absorbing armour (much like an armadillo's shell).

When I ran into him years later, I had been hoping for a devolution into flaccid middle-age, but his attitude couldn't have been cheerier and his physique couldn't have been more athletic. He had kept up with his swimming, he told me, and his two sons were following in his footsteps. A series of tricky life events had changed his outlook on life. He had become beautifully humble, charming and infectiously smiley. Goddamn it.

I played the game of blokeish conversation then made my excuses and drove home via the dairy. I purchased a packet of Cameo Creams and breathed them down whilst despairing about my life choices and general character and wishing I had been lucky enough to have been an Alpha Male Teenager.

HIKERS

There was an adult student I knew at university. Let's call him Steve. His everyday attire at lectures was hiking gear. He wore those streamlined black tights with one or two silver swirl lines running down along the thigh, with loose black shorts over the top of them, which were essentially useless because they were so flimsy. He had on thick woollen socks – those creamy ones with green flecks – bunched low around the ankle, and big tan boots where most of the laces were threaded through holes except at the top of the boot where they were woven around hooks. He'd wear a zip-up jacket made with some sort of technology that meant it could self-clean using his sweat. Around his neck wasn't a scarf but a cotton muff … is that the right word? In winter, he'd wear a woollen hat and fingerless gloves.

The lecture we took together was a two-hour affair. I think maybe those two hours intersected with his protein-eating regime because at some point during the lecture a Tupperware container containing nuts of some description would always come out.

Steve rode his bloody bike bloody everywhere. He was forever gliding it to a stop outside the lecture room and locking it up on the bike stand outside.

He was tanned and lean with not an ounce of fat on him. His hair was swept across his head and was nearly always sweaty from his various exertions. His calf muscles were huge, and I think he may have shaved his legs for the sake of aerodynamics.

I saw him maybe five times after we had completed our course together. Once he was on his bike. The four other times was on bushwalks around the city. I'm not much of a bushwalker. I've done bushwalks around Auckland maybe eight times and on half of those I encountered Steve. I don't know what that indicates about his bushwalking frequency.

Each time he was wearing those black tights with flimsy shorts over them, and he'd be running either down the slope towards me or coming up behind me. I'd be wheezing and panting, gripping the nearby trees for support and he'd race past, nodding at me without a trace of recognition in his eyes. Then he'd disappear around the next corner, with the only sweat being broken by him slicking his hair to his head.

I've since come across multiple other Steves. Every time I do some sort of bushy mountain climb, there they are. Men by themselves, dressed in all the gear, challenging themselves with yet another physical feat. They often cast their eyes over their streamlined wristwatches, seeing if they can exert themselves just that little bit more.

At the top of the hill, or whatever it is they're surmounting, they kick their legs out to get the lactic acid dissipating and take a chug on their streamlined, metallic drink bottles, which they usually have conveniently clipped to a streamlined part of their streamlined backpack or jacket. They barely look at the view as they shake their body out, before heading back down the hill, hoping to beat their personal best.

The only time I've done *hiking* hiking – the one where you take your big backpack with sleeping bag and tin plates and the knife/fork/spoon that clip together, and you stay in huts – was a three-day walk south of Palmerston North. It was there that I met a whole new breed of Hikers. I was by myself and noticed quite a few other young men doing the walk either by themselves or in pairs. They all wore the right gear. The nylony trousers, usually khaki coloured, that made the swish, swish, swish noise. They'd have nylony jackets with a peaked part on the hood, usually of rich blue but sometimes red, sometimes green. Underneath that they'd be wearing a grey woollen sweater. They all absolutely loved head torches and would have them on from an hour before dusk until just before they got into their sleeping bags.

There never seemed to be much joy in any of their demeanours. At the huts they were all very gracious to one another, speaking in hushed tones, but I could never exactly work out why they were even doing this walk. That was until I met a young man, let's call him Carl.

I arrived at a hut to find Carl and another young couple there. Soon more people arrived, and Carl was quick to loudly introduce himself to everyone who walked in.

I didn't think I had much to offer, being unfit and without any of the gear, but the next morning he suggested that he and I walk together for a bit. I agreed and he insisted on walking behind me.

Often, I found myself leaning against trees and rocks to catch my breath and pleading with him to go in front, but he said it was good for me to set the pace because he needed to take it a bit easier. He needed to stop racing and take time to appreciate his surroundings.

At lunch, we sat beside a river and he commented on the impracticality of all my food choices.

'Why would you bring bread on a hiking trip, bro?' he said as he offered me one of his protein bars.

As the day progressed, I tried to formulate an excuse not to walk with him the following day. I asked him why he hiked. He explained that it was an achievement thing. He wanted to tick off all the big walks in New Zealand. But why? Well, just for the sake of doing it. He also said, though not particularly eloquently, that there was a therapeutic aspect to it.

He'd had a terrible break-up where his girlfriend and best friend got together. After that he found going for long hikes gave him a chance to address all his feelings.

The next morning I managed to weasel out of walking with him. I said I wanted to leave after lunch (but left an hour after him). I mean, he was nice, but his pace was ridiculous.

FESTIVAL GOERS

Festivals, where people can be free to be themselves and just groove to the music, drink ciders and socialise, where they can dress up as Native Americans and wear their paper festival bracelets with pride. There are the day-long city festivals, sure, but the real treasures go to the weekend-long festivals in the middle of the wilderness.

There are three types of weekend-long Festival Goers who I have had the great pleasure of observing through my festival-going experiences. First, there is the girl who loves to get onto her boyfriend's shoulders whenever a crowd gathers.

You know the type. These days they wear big, floppy hats, singlets and frayed jean shorts. They're always perched up there, their thighs held in place by their boyfriend's muscular hands, with a smug smile on their face. They secretly love everyone looking up at them and they love that the band has a full view of them.

My irritation with them is that, if you're unlucky enough to be behind them, you won't be able to see the band play, but this good-looking couple doesn't give a shit about that.

Next up there are the everyday people who finally have an opportunity to get their fire poi out for a spin. If they don't have poi, they'll have those crazy stick things where it looks like they're juggling, but they're hitting the sticks from side to side. Do you know the things I'm talking about?

There was one particular fellow I noticed at a few festivals I attended. He had very pointed features and reddish dreadlocks, which he pulled back into a ponytail that stuck out horizontally from the back of his head. Regardless of the weather, he would wear a leathery waistcoat, usually of a reddish/maroonish persuasion, and nothing else on his torso. He was a fire breather.

As other festival goers milled around, he would create a circle within them. He would then take what looked like a big burning marshmallow on a stick and spit at it to cause a huge eruption of fire. His girlfriend, similarly dreadlocked but with ponytails sprouting from the top of her head, would then do a fire poi routine.

Every time I watched them doing this routine, which was basically the same every time, I scanned the surrounding group and noted that the facial expressions of the onlookers barely changed from before the fire breathing to during the fire breathing. This feat of pyrotechnic mastery appeared to have no effect on them. I thought. 'Come on guys, give these dreadlocked performers a bit of enthusiasm!'

After one of their performances, I sidled up to the dreadlocked couple to find out the lay of their land. They were a lovely couple who enjoyed compliments about their performances. Well, he did. She seemed blasé about the whole thing. I asked if they were hired by the festivals to perform. He told me that occasionally they were, but usually they just enjoyed having an opportunity to do what they did best.

Finally, I need to mention the packs of young, straight male Festival Goers. For many years I attended the Splore Festival about an hour out of Auckland. It was three days of non-stop dancing, fairy lights strung through pohutukawa trees, drinking craft beers and wearing animal onesies.

Within the sea of writhing bodies, there was always – ALWAYS – a group of boys who would get up on the DJ stand and dance, looking out over everyone else. They were invariably intoxicated and not completely sure where they were or what was happening. They would clump around the DJ stand or the band on stage and completely block everyone else's view. Some of them didn't even dance with much enthusiasm. They were simply up on stage swaying whilst blocking everyone else's goddamn view of the performers they actually wanted to see.

I noticed one boy dancing on the stage, blocking my view of the DJ. He wore an open Hawaiian shirt and short shorts. About two hours later, I saw him dancing on another DJ's stage, blocking my view again, but this time he was looking around, confused. In his murky state, he couldn't find his friends.

We found him later, seated on a grassy knoll on the way to the Chill Out Zone. His elbows were on his knees and he was sobbing between dry retches. We asked if we could help. He told us he wanted to keep dancing, but he couldn't find his friends. We suggested that, as it was 4 am, maybe we should help him back to his tent because surely that was where all his friends would be. He seemed to agree.

The thing about this particular festival is it is on a beach/bay/cove, but the tenting area is up a huge hill, which gets muddier as the festival progresses. We walked with him up the hill, a laboriously tedious task, as he talked about being 'maggoted' then fell into some bracken.

When we finally reached the top, we had the challenge of finding his tent in literally 10 paddocks' worth of tents. Everywhere we walked he tripped over tent ropes before somehow managing to get caught up in the nylon walls, thereby waking the occupants.

He hovered outside one tent so we asked if it was his. He nodded enthusiastically. He tried to open the zip then tripped over nothing and slid down on the nylon. We opened the zip for him, and he crawled in amidst several confused campers. One of them stuck her head out and asked who we were and who the guy was.

We explained that he'd said it was his tent. At that, the girl seemed to give up caring and said good night. Thankfully for us, he'd found a place for the rest of the evening.

We saw him the next day, as bright as a daisy, dancing away and laughing with his new friends – the two girls he'd shared the tent with the night before. None of them recognised us. I told him that we'd helped him mere hours ago. He was very appreciative and kept hugging me.

That night, I saw him standing on the DJ stage, completely wasted, barely keeping in time to the music, blocking everyone's view.

HUNTERS

There was a brother and sister who lived down the road from my childhood home. My grandfather used to call them 'the butterballs' because of their larger girths.

The boy butterball was into hunting, as are a lot of boys in rural New Zealand. One of my earliest memories of him was him having a frenzy at the thought of killing possums. 'I hate them! I hate them so much! I want to kill them! I want to smash their brains! Gah! Kill! Kill! Kill!'

His canine teeth were showing and there was a crazed look in his eyes. He was about six at the time, but he had clearly been indoctrinated into the world of hunting.

Later, when I was part of Cubs (the younger version of Scouts) the powers-that-be organised a big hunt. It involved a weekend where you had to kill as many vermin as possible. I can still see the huge piles of carcasses outside the community hall – rats, rabbits, hares and possums of all descriptions.

The night the group of us Cubs and our dads went hunting, we travelled by ute, which had huge high-beam torches attached to the roof. I was on the back of the ute as we drove up to the thick bush of the Kaimai.

The ute was parked to face the trees, then the torches were turned on. They illuminated dozens of eyes. The rifles were fired and, one after another, the eyes disappeared in conjunction with a pained squeal. We collected all the carcasses together and put them in a pile on the back of the ute.

At one point, we discovered one of the shot possums had a living joey in its pouch. One of the fathers took a good look at the baby then killed it by jabbing his heavy boot down onto its skull in front of half a dozen boys. I looked at the other boys. Their faces had all blanched, but there was no other reaction. Now was not the time to show weakness.

We climbed back onto the ute, despite the heaviness in our stomachs, and drove onto the next slaughter zone. I watched the father who had killed the joey. I couldn't pick up any sort of regret or guilt about what he had just done. In fact, pretty soon after that, he was whooping and hollering with the other fathers. He was bloodthirsty.

Cut to two decades later. As an adult, I've spent far too much time looking over the national hunting magazines. Why? They are fascinating insights into a certain species of New Zealanders. Beaming out of these magazines' pages are the faces of men, and quite often women, wearing Swanndris and laced boots. They are either standing over a dead stag, holding the bloodied head upright by its antlers and giving a thumbs-up, or carrying a dead boar around their shoulders, holding it in place with one hand, and giving a thumbs-up with the other.

I'm fascinated by this breed of person. First off, they seem to easily manage to switch off any empathy for animals. Yet they still seem to be caring parents because many of the hunting magazine articles involve hunters teaching their children the tricks of the trade. In fact, most of these magazines have children's sections where they're taught how to use a Swiss Army Knife, or how to hog-tie an actual dead hog. I guess when you grow up with it, hunting becomes second nature. Maybe it's harking back to our origins. If we didn't have the ability to hunt, maybe we wouldn't be here today.

After thinking about it for a while, I decided to take up the next opportunity to go hunting with someone, not that the opportunity regularly arose. About a year later, an invitation came. An acquaintance was going duck hunting with some mates and I tagged along.

We arrived at a very boggy area and set up camp at a 'blind'. What followed was a lot of beer drinking and chewing the fat. There was constant ribbing and taking the piss out of each other, but they all seemed cautious about taking the piss out of me. I was up for a tease and teased them, but they all seemed too awkward to tease me back.

My favourite of them was a fellow we'll call Darryl. He was the shortest of the group, but he made up for it with all his hunting paraphernalia. He wore a camouflage outfit, which the others were merciless about, and rubber waders. He had a drinking canister that was also camouflage. That got a lot of ribbing. He had brought a net in case he needed to scoop a dead bird out of the water. He had a duck whistle and a duck decoy, which he set free into the water where it disappeared into some weeds, never to be found again.

Eventually some ducks did arrive, and all the rifles came up. Everyone managed to bring down a duck except Darryl, who simply muttered 'Damn it!' every time he fired his rifle.

The day progressed and I was offered a rifle to shoot, but I politely declined, thereby furthering my distance between me and the men.

Darryl, meanwhile, had his own problems to worry about. He still hadn't hit a duck. The best shot amongst them managed to bring down six, and the other two had brought down three each.

At one point, Darryl thought he'd shot one, but it had actually been one of the other guys. The other guy decided to keep quiet about it. Darryl was so excited. He ran over with his net to fetch the duck. Thankfully, he was wearing his waders because he put a foot wrong and glided into the water in the most ungainly of fashions – but none of the others laughed.

When he returned, his jubilation had gone. He had thought it all through and worked out that the brutal death couldn't have been at his hands, so he handed the duck over to its rightful shooter. The other three insisted it had been Darryl who had shot it, but he refused to believe it.

By the end of the day, all the joking and ribbing had gone. Everyone felt sorry for Darryl, but he remained chipper.

'Next time,' he said, as he used the water from his camouflage drinking canister to wash away the weed from his waders. 'Next time ...'

THE WORLDLY NEW ZEALANDER

There is a breed of New Zealander out there who looks down on New Zealand and always references how everything is done so much better overseas, especially in Europe. God, they love Europe. They look on New Zealand as crass, low class, basic and terribly unsophisticated.

I've met a few of these Worldly New Zealanders in my time but the most extreme was a fellow I'm going to call Sebastian, who lived in downtown Wellington. He looked European. He was slim and loved crisp, white shirts and neckerchiefs. He also loved loafers, or some other such shoes without socks. He was a New Zealander, but his accent was some sort of British hybrid.

Sebastian was always taking long sojourns to France. He was fluent in French and Italian, but didn't broadcast that fact, even though he liked everyone to know it. He also seemed to know everyone of importance, yes in New Zealand, but internationally as well.

'That was like the time I met Elton,' Sebastian said.

'Elton?' I asked.

'Yah.'

'Elton John?'

'Yes.'

'You've met Elton John?!' I blurted.

'I spent the whole weekend with him in Majorca.' Then he shrugged like it was no big deal. This was quickly followed by, 'Oh my god! I've run out of Perrier …'

'I'm going to the supermarket soon. Do you want me to get some?' I asked.

He looked at me with pity. I read his facial expression as saying, 'Oh you poor, pathetic country boy.'

Then he said, 'I don't go to the supermarket.'

To this day, I still don't know where he gets his food from.

Oh, and when it comes to food, he is out of control. His meals are so exquisite you wouldn't be surprised if every individual ingredient cost $100 each. I can't imagine this guy ever eating a cheap pie, bakery sandwich or chocolate bar.

I made the mistake not once, not twice, but thrice of deciding where we would eat a meal together. His disdain and disappointment were evident from the moment we stepped into each of the various establishments.

He would look over the menus, using as little surface area of his fingers as possible to turn the pages. He'd then ask the waiter for a specific meal as nothing on the menu matched his tastes. Invariably, the waiter couldn't provide what he wanted, so he'd settle for an entree instead of a main meal, which he'd just pick at.

Afterwards I would apologise for the sub-par quality of the dining experience, and he would answer, not very convincingly, that it was absolutely fine.

How the Wordly New Zealander can afford this lifestyle I can't work out. How can he afford all this travel to France? His parents must pay for everything. After all, they'd bought him a loft in the middle of Wellington – a huge expansive number with a grand piano in the spacious living room/dining room area. He could play it, of course, and sing. He sings beautifully, according to people at his dinner parties.

The last dinner party of his I attended was before he set off to Europe permanently. I made the mistake of bringing a $27 bottle of white wine. At the time, that was so expensive for me. He told me he wasn't going to let me drink that 'rubbish' and told me to get the French red from the top of the walk-in pantry.

Inside the pantry I did a quick inventory, opening all the cupboards and looking over all the shelves. There were multiple packets of crazily shaped pasta with labels entirely in Italian. There were multiple bottles of Italian olive oil. There were rows of Perrier water and Orangino, or whatever it's called. There was nothing made in New Zealand, and there was nothing much that would have cost less than $100. I hoped to see some sign that this guy was a fraud, but he seemed to be the real deal.

I got the French red and re-emerged to find him talking about various celebrities like they were close friends of his. He mentioned the time he did drugs with Rupert Everett, and the time he hung out with Uma Thurman and her brother. 'Lovely people. Bonkers, but lovely people.'

Later in the evening, as we were enjoying his skillet cod with lemon and capers – being vegetarian, he'd made me a tofu version; he acted like it was a slight burden, but loved it when I praised him copiously – he dropped into conversation that he was a baronet. A what?

A baronet. It sounded fancy, but I didn't know what it meant. He shrugged like it was no big deal and explained that a baronet was the lowest rung of the royal family, but it still warranted him being a 'Sir'.

I nodded, disbelieving. I mean, if he was a member of the royal family then that might explain how he could afford his extravagant lifestyle. But what was he doing in little old New Zealand? The whole thing, this whole world he had created for himself, seemed a tad too fantastical.

When he left for Europe, we didn't keep in contact. It wasn't until I was visiting London that I decided to flick him a message to see if he would be interested in a drink together. I suggested a pub, but he invited me to an exclusive club where you could only get in if you were a member.

I met him outside the club, and he was a little distant. His faux English accent was now through the roof. As we headed up the elevator he bragged incessantly. He told me he'd hung out with the pop star Adele. Apparently, she liked him because he was so down-to-earth and matter-of-fact. He also told me I should be excited because Orlando Bloom was often seen at the club we were about to walk into.

I felt quite intimidated. The club was low-lit, with a hodgepodge of different couches, armchairs and pot plants. People were lounging everywhere, looking casual yet so fancy.

Sebastian made a show of walking up to several of the punters, air-kissing them on both cheeks and chatting away. He introduced me to these people, but they weren't all that interested in me.

We bought some drinks – I offered to pay, and he didn't put up much of a fight – then we found a spare couch. A young woman wearing pearls leaned over the back of the chair to talk to Sebastian in a very intimate fashion. As I nursed my drink, I eavesdropped, of course.

The woman talked about her life and her problems, and Sebastian couldn't get a word in. He could have been anyone to her; he was just a listening ear. After the conversation, he turned back to me with an eager smile.

'So, this is your life now?' I asked. 'It's so great.'

'Isn't it? It's hard to keep all the socialising and the work going, but I've made some great friends.'

His mouth was smiling but his eyes certainly weren't. He looked away quickly.

The club was still going hard at midnight, but I had to leave London early the next morning, so I made my excuses to leave. He walked me to the elevator and said how lovely it was to catch up and that I must make contact next time I was in town. He then nodded to a man in a suit and top hat standing by the elevator, who proceeded to push the elevator button on my behalf.

My worldly friend then gave me a hug that lingered. It felt like he was really holding on to me. As we disengaged, he was quick to smile.

'Are you okay?' I asked.

'Yes, of course. It's just very hard when you've moved to

a new country, but it's great. Anyway, you should go. Have a good trip tomorrow.'

The elevator arrived and I stepped into it. We waved as the doors closed and that was that. I haven't heard from him since, but often think of him when I'm hosting a dinner party. His judging gaze haunts me as I select the various ingredients, urging me to choose with as much sophistication as I can muster.

OVERSEAS KIWIS

When I think of Overseas Kiwis, I instantly think of those wonderful ambassadors for the country who love to get maggoted at the various Walkabout pubs throughout Britain. They hang out exclusively with other New Zealanders and take photos doing gangster signs outside Auschwitz. They then return home to New Zealand having not really taken in any of the nuances of other cultures. Their overseas sojourn was simply a succession of visits to amazing adventure playgrounds where all their whims could be indulged. And I love them for it.

There are also those New Zealanders who live overseas because New Zealand never 'got them'. I knew one 'artist' who liked to do various sculptures in Auckland, which involved tipped-over plastic chairs and buckets. These exhibitions left you thinking, 'Is this the actual artwork or have I stumbled into the janitor's closet?'

Years later, I met this Overseas Kiwi in Berlin, where he was the toast of the town. He was living his best life, exhibiting his work to very appreciative audiences, who could clearly see that the tipped-over plastic chair represented domestic abuse.

He introduced me to a collective of expat fine artists, musicians and performers, and they were having the time of their lives in Berlin – and somehow getting paid for it. They were living in a culture where the common man invested in the arts. There, your bricklayer attended obscure puppet shows and your butcher attended folk music gigs in craft beer pubs.

All of these Overseas Kiwis had the attitude that back home in New Zealand they were scorned or ridiculed. In reality, now they had had a little success overseas, they were suddenly appreciated back in Aotearoa, but they weren't planning on going back any time soon.

This phenomenon isn't only connected with the arts scene, unfortunately. I met lawyers, entrepreneurs and teachers who had achieved much greater success than they'd had at home in New Zealand. Their success may have had something to do with coming from a culture where the class system isn't so inherently ingrained. When living in Europe – and especially in Britain – our host country can't necessarily pigeonhole us, so it's easier for us to navigate the various social strata unimpeded.

This all raises two issues. First of all, New Zealand is so small that it can't really maintain a thriving arts scene, nor is there much scope for success in other fields – except rugby. Male rugby. But also, if anyone excels in anything overseas, they are suddenly feted as being of worth here and we are quick to claim them as our own. But, whilst still in New Zealand, these people were largely ignored, or, heaven forbid, if they'd been confident in their skills, then we would have mercilessly torn them down to size. How dare they express how good they are? That's definitely not how it's done here.

'Who does he think he is? He's not that good.'

'Look at her. She's so far up herself it's not even funny.'

On a more positive note, Kiwis abroad have a reputation as being very good workers. I worked at a costume store in London for a year. Fifteen extra staff were hired in the month leading up to Halloween and were distributed over the store's three floors.

The top floor was dedicated to female costumes. In the lead-up to Halloween, these included Sexy Bee, Strumpet Nurse, Horny Banana Girl and 'Sex-starved Slut'. The outfits invariably had some sort of suspenders going on, a tutu or some other tiny skirt, a figure-hugging singlet or tank top exposing the wearer's stomach and devil's horns or bee antennae to top it off with a flourish. Basically, if you weren't size zero, or didn't have extreme confidence, I don't know why you'd buy them, let alone wear them.

The next floor down was the men's costumes. This was where I was designated. There were shelves upon shelves of plastic bags containing crappily made costumes that would end up in landfill after one wear.

There were many horny ones, like Camel Toe Carol, Pearl Necklace and 'my huge foam balls are hanging down beneath the bottom of my shorts and that is the entirety of the costume'. There were also the grotesque zombies and Frankenstein's monsters, which a lot of plus-size women were forced to wear because the Sexy Bee costume could barely fit their foot.

Then there were the just useless costumes like the nerd costume, for example. This contained cheaply made black pants, a cheaply made white T-shirt and plastic glasses with a fake Band-aid wrapped around the bridge. Couldn't you just make that costume with things you found lying around the house? Honestly, it was all such crap.

The bottom floor was dedicated to terrible-quality props – fake cigars, tacky pearl necklaces, plastic glasses that magnify your eyes but have flimsy handles, moustaches that didn't even look like moustaches and fell off with only the slightest of upper-lip sweat.

Anyway, each of the three floors got five employees to deal with the Halloween rush. Each of those three groups of five had one Kiwi, so there was one Kiwi working on each floor. Once the craziness of Halloween had passed, each floor was allowed to keep one employee to stay until after New Year. The three selected were the three Kiwis.

When we found this out, we were all in the staffroom completely confused. None of us felt like we'd done a particularly good job. I'd spent a lot of time pretending to look for costumes 'out the back' when I was actually writing a play on the back of old receipts. The Kiwi girl in the women's section tried on every single one of the costumes and had hundreds of photos to show for her efforts. And the young Kiwi guy, on the 'terrible-quality props' floor, took three toilet breaks a day for a minimum of 10 minutes each.

I asked my floor manager why the three of us had been selected. She told me it was because the other employees had been so lazy, were never at work on time and had terrible attitudes. I stared at her for a moment, trying to mask my surprise. My god, these other guys must've been absolute shit.

CONCLUSION

And there you go. Just like that, we've finished.

Yes, I know, I've missed so many character types. I didn't know where to slot the person who goes over receipts meticulously, hoping they've been overcharged and can make a fuss about it. I didn't mention the type of person whose greatest satisfaction is when a peanut butter container is completely used up with not a crumb of peanut left. And I didn't even think about the overweight music fan, who is always at gigs with big sweat circles under his armpits, permanent stubble and unkempt hair plastered across his forehead as he rocks it out.

All I can do is hope that I've captured an essence of the cast of characters who make up New Zealand. But then I wonder if any of these character types are truly 'New Zealand'? Stingy people exist the world over. Rough sleeping and homelessness are the plight of all of humanity. An obsession with the zodiac exists throughout the world. Even rugby fans have their equivalents in all other sporting codes the world over.

This begs the question, what makes somebody a New Zealander? A recent immigrant from another country, who has been given New Zealand citizenship, is just as much a

New Zealander as someone who was born here. This is true even if they haven't had the chance to develop all of our idiosyncrasies.

For some people, a true 'New Zealander' is of Pakeha or Maori descent with family who have been here for generations. But Chinese people have been here for many generations, as have Pacific Islanders. We're such a melting pot and kinda always have been.

On a side note, I decided not to delve too much into the topic of different races because, let's face it, who am I, a privileged white man, to talk in detail about people of different ethnicities and the nuances of their cultures when I'm just observing from afar? That's why I decided to focus on the more universal human personality traits. I hope that's okay. Gulp.

What are some of the absolute givens of living in New Zealand?

We live on some islands. We don't have any dangerous native animals living here.

Maori lived here for generations before the Europeans arrived. Starting out as a port of call for whalers and sealers, Europeans then tried to tame the land whilst the British aggressively colonised the place. It became the home for quite a few impoverished Europeans for a time. It took a long time to shake off some of that colonial influence. In my grandparents' generation, many Pakeha still called Great Britain home, no matter how many generations ago their ancestors moved here.

We are primary producers. We export food to the rest of the world. Is the fact that we produce food for other, bigger countries something that affects our ethos? Are we snivelling, pathetic little siblings to the big players? Or is there a smugness within us, knowing that if all the world turns to shit, we've got all our cows and plum trees here. We are so damned isolated we could potentially be the best place to live. I mean, even Shania Twain bought land in New Zealand on the off-chance civilisation as we knew it ended, and she could live here comfortably. (Instead, she got divorced and the land is now owned by her ex-husband.)

In the 1970s dystopian sci-fi novel, *The Chrysalids*, New Zealand (called Zealand in the novel because they've ditched the 'New') is the only country to escape a nuclear holocaust. It has become a technologically advanced society where everyone communicates using telepathy whilst they fly everywhere in helicopters.

Back to the modern day, and it wasn't that long ago that Maori children were given a slap with a ruler if they spoke their language. Now, though, te reo has made a huge resurgence with free courses being offered and various words being incorporated into everyday vernacular, further colouring New Zealand's uniqueness.

There's always been a huge back and forth between New Zealand and the Pacific Islands, with Auckland becoming the city with the largest population of Pasifika people in the world. Many people of other ethnicities have also moved here, and they've brought with them certain ingredients that combine to make up the New Zealand psyche.

We were renowned for our social welfare system after World War Two and were considered something of a utopia. We then plunged into capitalism in a big way and were affected by the stock market crash of the 1980s.

For years, we've been subjected to a lot of English and American culture through TV and films. During my childhood, the sitcom *Friends* had a huge impact on the way we spoke and how we looked at ourselves. When New Zealand started making its own television content, everyone would cringe at the accents. Cultural cringe became a huge thing for us, as did the Tall Poppy Syndrome, which involved cutting down those who excelled above the rest.

Our cities have often been in lists of the 'top cities to live' in the world, sometimes topping the list, sometimes being second or third behind Vancouver or Melbourne or some such delightful city. Even our accent was voted the sexiest at one point.

With all that bubbling beneath, has that dictated anything specific about how we act and behave? Or are we just a collection of DNA and instincts developed over millions of years in Africa, where social beings that had to rely on each other to survive against sabre-toothed tigers were created? Is every behaviour we express simply a way to survive both on an animalistic level and on a social level? I mean, no one likes being ostracised from a group, and maybe those inherent behaviours are simply being manifested by each and every one of the eight billion or so people in the world right now.

Can people even be categorised? Are we all hugely unique? Can we change our personalities or are they fixed forever? Anyway, these were the thoughts that were constantly churning through my head as I attempted to write this book.

Now, at the end of it, I don't think I've answered any of these questions for myself. All that's happened is I've fallen further in love with human nature as a whole – and it is that love that has made this so much fun to write. I'm so grateful to have had the opportunity to collate my observations about my absolute favourite topic – human beings. I hope you've enjoyed the ride with me.

Cheers and much love,
Tom Sainsbury (An Irritable Dad meets a Social Media Kiwi with just a touch of an Apologist for Existing) XX